OUTDOORLIFE

URBAN SURVIVAL GUIDE

TOP URBAN SURVIVAL SKILLS

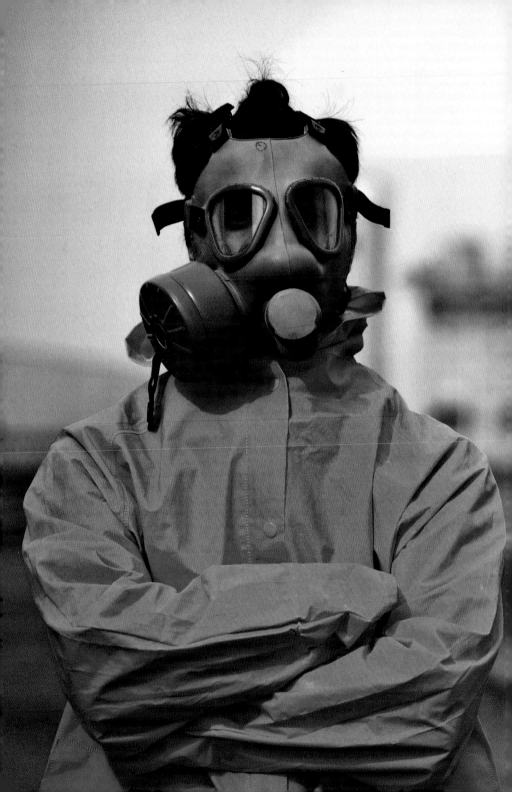

OUTDOORLIFE

URBAN SURVIVAL GUIDE

TOP URBAN SURVIVAL SKILLS

RICH JOHNSON
AND THE EDITORS OF *OUTDOOR LIFE*

weldonowen

CONTENTS

Dear Reader,

Great news! You're reading this book, and that means you must be alive. Which means you're following my **NUMBER ONE RULE** for survival: Stay alive. So far, so good. I can tell you're going to be a good student.

RULE NUMBER TWO Attitude trumps everything else. If your brain's not in the game, the rest of you will suffer for it. Survival is mental— and I'm not talking about your education, I'm talking about your mindset. As important as it is to know proper survival techniques, if your attitude stinks, you're probably not going to make it. Eliminate the word "quit" from your vocabulary. QUIT is a four-letter word, and around here we don't talk like that (unless a bear is gnawing on us).

RULE NUMBER THREE Don't take avoidable risks. Always look for the safest path, and pace yourself to prevent injuries. Do the things you want to do—but be smart about how you do them.

RULE NUMBER FOUR Live with integrity—and a big part of that is caring about others. Find ways to help people through rough spots. Lift those who need lifting; someday you'll need lifting, too.

RULE NUMBER FIVE Continually work to better your situation, especially if it's dodgy. Even small improvements to comfort or security will improve your spirits. And possibly save your bacon.

MY PHILOSOPHY IN A NUTSHELL To give yourself the best chance for survival, fill your head with accurate information, fill your hands with skill, and fill your life with experience. Let wisdom be your guide and common sense your pattern.

Take care out there,

Rich John

✚ SURVIVAL STRATEGIES

KNOW WHAT'S HAPPENING Problems arise when you don't pay attention. If you're cognizant of your surroundings, you can respond appropriately.

PRIORITIZE Once you know what kind of fix you're in, decide what your most pressing need is. If your buddy has a bullet in his leg, your most pressing need isn't hunting dinner.

DEVISE A PLAN Now that you know what needs to be done first (and next, and then next), decide how to attack the problem. Weigh your options, then make smart decisions that will give you the desired result.

GO TO WORK The time has come for the rubber to meet the road. As you work on resolving each challenge, continually assess the situation. Decide if what you're doing is working, or if you need to change strategies.

Remember, you're trying to survive, and that's a worthy goal if ever there was one. Give it your all and good luck!

1 CHECKLIST
Assemble a Home Survival Kit

Outdoor adventurers know not to venture into the wild without the necessary survival gear. But what about when you're at home? Or out running errands? No matter where you are, you should always have certain survival essentials at hand. And while there's no such thing as a universal "bug-out bag" (called a "BOB" for short), you can assemble a variety of kits for every situation.

Start off by putting together the items below to create a fully stocked at-home kit that can meet the your needs and those of your family in a disaster scenario. Store it someplace accessible so that you're always at the ready.

- ☐ Nonperishable food (a three-day supply for each person)
- ☐ Small stove with propane or other fuel
- ☐ Kitchen accessories and cooking utensils
- ☐ Can opener
- ☐ Three-day supply of water (1 gallon/3.75 l per person, per day)
- ☐ Water-purification tablets
- ☐ Bleach (add to water to make a mild disinfectant, or use 16 drops per gallon/3.75 l to purify water)
- ☐ Portable, battery-powered radio or television and extra batteries
- ☐ Flashlight and extra batteries
- ☐ Battery-operated, hand-cranked, or solar-powered cell-phone charger
- ☐ Tools, such as a wrench for shutting off utilities, a screwdriver, and a hammer
- ☐ First-aid kit and manual
- ☐ Sanitation and hygiene items, such as soap, moist towelettes, toilet paper, and towels
- ☐ Items for infants, such as formula, diapers, bottles, and pacifiers
- ☐ Signal mirror and whistle
- ☐ Extra clothing for each person, including a jacket, coat, long pants, and long-sleeved shirt
- ☐ Hat, mittens, scarf, or any other climate-appropriate clothing for each person
- ☐ Sturdy hiking boots or athletic shoes and socks
- ☐ Sleeping bag or warm blanket for each person
- ☐ Special-needs items, such as prescription medications, eyeglasses, contact lens solution, and hearing aid batteries
- ☐ Photocopies of credit and identification cards
- ☐ Cash and coins in small denominations
- ☐ Plastic bags in various sizes
- ☐ Ground cloth or tarp
- ☐ Powdered, chlorinated lime to treat waste and discourage insects
- ☐ Strike-anywhere matches in a waterproof container

2 Stock an Office BOB

Disaster can strike at any time, including when you're at work. That's why it's smart to keep a BOB in your office or under your desk. It should include a set of rugged clothes (because scaling a wall in a suit is rarely a good idea), athletic shoes and socks (have you ever tried running in heels?), and a few food items and bottles of water. Toss everything in a single grab-and-go tote so you can evacuate efficiently, and then stash it in a drawer and forget about it. You'll be thankful to have it should your work environment ever become truly unpleasant.

3 CHECKLIST
Gear Up with a To-Go BOB

If you have to grab one bag and run because the world is caving in, that bag had better contain what you need for short-term survival. And since most of us evacuate in our cars, it's a good idea to keep this bag in your trunk, along with crucial road-safety items.

- ☐ Energy bars, trail mix, and a couple of separately packaged, ready-to-eat meals
- ☐ Several bottles of water, a filter, and water-purification tablets
- ☐ Tent and sleeping bag
- ☐ Fire striker, basic lighter, and tinder
- ☐ One entire change of clothing (such as pants, shirt, socks, underwear, gloves, hat, windbreaker, and poncho)
- ☐ Flashlight and extra batteries
- ☐ Knife and spork
- ☐ Military-grade can opener

- ☐ Heavy cord, snare wire, and fishing lures
- ☐ Battery-operated radio
- ☐ Battery-operated, hand-cranked, or solar-powered cell-phone charger
- ☐ First-aid kit and manual
- ☐ Sanitation and hygiene items, such as toilet paper, soap, and a small towel
- ☐ Special needs items, such as medications, eyeglasses, contact lens solutions, and hearing aid batteries
- ☐ Signal mirror and whistle

- ☐ Any car safety items, such as a spare tire, a tire iron, jumper cables, a windshield scraper, and hazard flares, plus any needed winter items (a small collapsible shovel, tire chains, and a bag of kitty litter)

4

CHECKLIST
Make a Kit in a Can

You can pack a surprising amount of crucial gear in a very small container—even one as small as a mint tin—to create a highly portable BOB that fits in your backpack. Check military surplus stores for ideal containers (grenade canisters work nicely), and stock the following items:

- ☐ Small pen and paper
- ☐ First-aid instruction cards
- ☐ Duct tape
- ☐ Razor blades
- ☐ Wire saw
- ☐ Waterproof matches or fire starters

- ☐ Needle and thread
- ☐ Safety pins
- ☐ Water-purification tablets
- ☐ Zip ties
- ☐ Adhesive bandages
- ☐ Disinfectant wipes

- ☐ Micro compass
- ☐ Fishing kit (ten hooks, four split shot, two swivels, 25 feet [7.6 m] of 20-pound [9-kg] test line)
- ☐ Folded one-page guide to edible plants in your area

- ☐ 5 square feet (0.5 sq m) of aluminum foil
- ☐ Signal mirror
- ☐ Bouillon cubes
- ☐ Shoelaces
- ☐ Copper wire
- ☐ AA batteries
- ☐ Alcohol swabs
- ☐ Painkillers

5

STEP-BY-STEP
Stop Bleeding

No one likes to see blood coming out of someone's body—least of all his or her own. Don't just cover it up: It's pressure that stops the bleeding.

STEP ONE Find the source of the bleeding. Got multiple cuts? Then deal with the worst first.

STEP TWO Put a sterile compress on the wound and apply firm pressure. If the cut is on an extremity, press both sides of the limb to keep it from bending back and away from the pressure.

STEP THREE If the compress soaks through, put another one over it and maintain pressure. Keep on stacking bandages until the bleeding has stopped.

STEP FOUR Remove the compresses and flush the wound with water to clean.

6

STEP-BY-STEP
Disinfect a Wound

Knowing how to disinfect a wound can be critical. Even small cuts can become infected, especially out in the wilderness. And if your body has to fight an infection, it diverts resources away from your overall health, leaving you susceptible to other illnesses.

STEP ONE Stop the bleeding and assess the injury. If the bleeding won't stop, or if the wound is so deep that it will need stitches, seek medical attention. If you're going to the hospital, don't bother with cleaning the wound. Leave that to a pro.

STEP TWO Flush the wound with clean water. Don't use hydrogen peroxide or alcohol; they can damage healthy tissue.

STEP THREE Thoroughly saturate the injury with a triple antibiotic ointment before applying a clean, dry dressing.

7 CHECKLIST
Build a First-Aid Kit

If you're the type of person who's always asking for a bandage or an aspirin, it's time to get it together. Make a kit that includes the following items:

- ☐ Aloe vera gel
- ☐ Scissors
- ☐ Nonadhesive dressing
- ☐ Medical tape
- ☐ Gauze roller bandages
- ☐ Anti-inflammatory drugs
- ☐ Antibacterial ointment
- ☐ Elastic roller bandages
- ☐ Surgical scrub brush

- ☐ Disinfectant towelettes
- ☐ Arm sling
- ☐ Splint material, such as an inflatable splint or a rigid splint made of wood, plastic, or other material
- ☐ Sterile compress
- ☐ Tweezers
- ☐ Selection of adhesive bandages, including butterfly bandages

8 Bandage a Wound

It takes 72 hours for skin to close up and become airtight. For small cuts and scrapes, just keep the area clean. For large cuts, you will probably have to do a little bit more.

DON'T STITCH IT UP We've all seen our action heroes use a needle and thread. Unless you have sterile sutures, a suture needle, and a tool to get the hook through the skin, this option isn't happening. (Likewise, leave sterilizing and closing a wound with a hot knife blade to the stars on the big screen.)

BUTTERFLY IT The best way to close a wound is to apply sterile adhesive strips after disinfecting it. First, line up the edges of the cut. Then, starting in the center of the wound, place an adhesive strip's end on one side of the cut. As you lay the strip across the wound, push the wound's edges together. Apply these bandages in a crisscross pattern down the length of the cut to keep the sides in contact, then dress with a sterile wrap.

BE SUPER In a pinch, superglue can hold your skin closed—it worked for soldiers in the Vietnam War. Just make sure you coat only the outside edges of the cut, not in the cut itself.

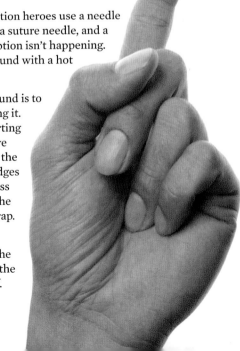

ASSESS AND RESPOND
Deal with Blood Loss

When you're in the outdoors, many objects you encounter will be pointed, jagged, or razor-sharp. Your tender human flesh doesn't stand a chance against a misdirected axe or an errant blade, and that doesn't even begin to take into account accidents involving sharp rocks, or a skin-shredding tumble on a

OOZE An abrasion or common scrape tears open capillaries, resulting in a slow trickle of blood from the wound. Infection is your biggest threat here.

- Disinfect the wound.

- Use moderate pressure to stop the bleeding.

- Keep the wound moist with aloe vera or antibiotic ointment until it has healed.

- Cover it with a semipermeable dressing.

- Change the dressing daily and inspect the wound for infection, which might require professional treatment.

SPURT If bright red blood shoots from the wound, you have arterial bleeding, and it's highly dangerous. Forget disinfecting; just stop the bleeding.

- Elevate the injury above the heart.

- Aggressively apply pressure.

- If a wound on a limb won't stop bleeding, tie a tourniquet above the wound and tighten it until the blood stops flowing. But be warned that the use of a tourniquet can lead to the necessity for amputation. Use one only when you must.

- Call 911 or transport the victim to an available medical facility immediately.

trail. So it's little surprise that blood-loss injuries are the most common afflictions in outdoor situations. Since there's a whole world of possible damage you can do to yourself out there, here are four common categories of bleeding and what to do for each.

FLOW If dark red blood gushes steadily, a vein has been opened. You've got to clean the wound and stop the flow until you can get the victim to a hospital.

· Elevate the injury above the heart.

· Use tweezers to remove any debris that is lodged in the cut. Disinfect the wound.

· Apply direct pressure to the injury. You can apply pressure with bare hands at first, but then search for something to serve as a direct-pressure pad.

· After the bleeding stops, use tape or cloth strips to secure the dressing over the wound.

INTERNAL If someone has been in a high-speed automobile accident or if a sharp object hit near an organ, he or she may be bleeding on the inside.

· Monitor for hypovolemia (a state in which blood levels are drastically reduced). Shock, pallor, rapid breathing, confusion, and lack of urine are all signs.

· Incline the victim toward the injured side. This constrains the blood flow to the damaged area, and keeps the good side up and running.

· Stabilize the victim, treat for shock, and call 911 or transport the victim to a medical facility immediately.

10

STEP-BY-STEP
Immobilize an Arm Injury

If you've injured an arm (with a fracture, a severe sprain, or an especially gnarly cut), you'll need to immobilize it for a while. Fashioning a sling is pretty straightforward, but it's a core bit of knowledge to have at your disposal; in particular, use this method if you're out in the wild and away from medical care.

STEP ONE Start with a square cloth approximately 3 by 3 feet (1 m by 1 m). Lay the cloth out flat, then fold it once diagonally to make a triangle.

STEP TWO Slip the injured arm into the fold, and bring both ends up around the neck, slanting the forearm up slightly.

STEP THREE Tie the corners in a knot. Gravity will naturally pull the forearm in its sling back down to a parallel position.

STEP FOUR Use a belt to immobilize the arm against the body. Wrap it around the chest, above the forearm but away from the problematic zone. Cinch it closed but not too tightly, to avoid cutting off circulation to the injured arm.

11

STEP-BY-STEP
Make a Splint

If someone injures a leg in the wild, immobilization is key—but you still have to walk back to civilization, so staying still isn't an option. So craft a splint with a sleeping pad, cardboard, or other flexible material.

STEP ONE Stop any bleeding with direct pressure.

STEP TWO Check for a pulse below the fracture and look at the skin—if it's pale, circulation may be cut off and you may need to set the bone (see above)

12 Set a Bone

Getting to a hospital is always the best recourse when dealing with broken bones, but if medical attention isn't readily available and blood isn't circulating to the limb, setting the bone might be the only way to save that arm or leg.

ASSESS THE BREAK Many breaks don't need setting, but a few, such as transverse, oblique, or impacted fractures, might. If the bone is protruding from the skin, don't try to set it. Just immobilize it.

CHECK FOR BLOOD FLOW Press on the skin below the fracture site. The skin should turn white and then quickly return to pink. Pale or bluish skin, numbness, tingling, or the lack of a pulse in the limb indicate a loss of circulation, and you need to set the bone to restore blood flow.

PUT IT IN PLACE To reduce swelling, pain, and tissue damage from lack of circulation, carefully pull in opposite directions on both sides of the break to realign the bone.

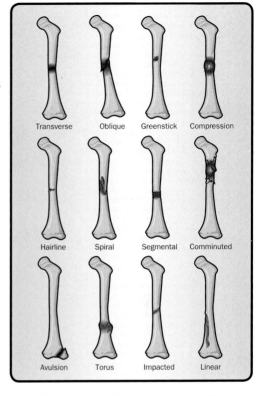

Transverse   Oblique   Greenstick   Compression

Hairline   Spiral   Segmental   Comminuted

Avulsion   Torus   Impacted   Linear

STEP THREE Slide the unfolded splint material beneath the limb, and pad it for comfort and stability.

STEP FOUR Fold the splint around the leg, securing it with elastic, gauze, or other material. The splint should be tight enough to keep the bone from shifting, but it should not impair circulation. If the break involves a joint, secure the splint both above and below it for extra stability.

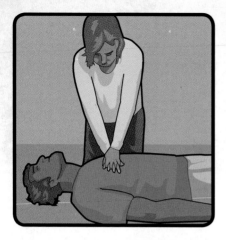

13

STEP-BY-STEP
Save with CPR

It's an absolute nightmare: Someone in your group loses his or her pulse and quits breathing, and it's up to you to get blood flowing to the heart and brain. The mere thought of this scenario should convince you to get trained in cardiopulmonary resuscitation (CPR). But if you're untrained, you can still do some good. Here's how.

STEP ONE Call 911. This is life or death, and you should get medics on the scene as soon as possible.

STEP TWO Place the heel of your hand in the middle of the victim's chest (just a bit above the bottom of the sternum) and stack your other hand on top of the first.

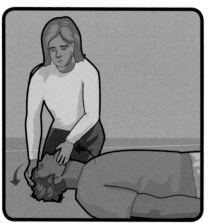

STEP THREE Begin compressions on the victim's chest, pushing 2 inches (5 cm) down. Keep your elbows locked, and for an adult victim, put your full weight over him or her—the more force, the better.

STEP FOUR Pump at a rate of 100 beats per minute, continuing until help arrives or the victim recovers. If other people are nearby, take turns performing compressions, as the effort will easily tire you out after awhile.

STEP FIVE If you are certified in CPR, stop after 30 compressions and gently tilt back the victim's head in order to open up his or her airway.

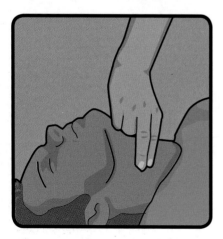

STEP SIX Again, only if you're certified, pinch the victim's nose shut. Seal your mouth over his or hers, and give two deep breaths. Continue to repeat the entire process until help arrives or the victim recovers.

14 STEP-BY-STEP
Perform the Heimlich Maneuver

A choking victim can't tell you what's wrong or how to help him or her. Usually, people with a constricted airway will wrap their hands around their throat, but it's up to you to recognize the situation and act fast. Here's how to help if you're dealing with an adult.

STEP ONE Stand behind the victim and place one arm around the waist. Put your fist below the ribs but above the navel with your thumb resting against the stomach.

STEP TWO Wrap your other arm around the victim's waist and cover your fist with the palm of this hand.

STEP THREE Press your fist into the abdomen with quick, upward thrusts. Don't press on the rib cage, and try to keep the force of your thrusts in your hands, not your arms.

STEP FOUR Repeat the abdominal thrusts until the object is dislodged and the airway has been cleared.

If you can't reach around the victim's waist, or if he or she is unconscious, move the person to a supine position on the floor and perform the Heimlich maneuver while straddling the victim's legs or hips.

15 Fake a Sling

No sling? No problem. When it comes to immobilizing an arm, just about any kind of cloth or material can work, so look around. For instance, you can place a loop of rope or a belt loosely around the neck, slide the arm into it so that the wrist rests inside the loop, knot or cinch the rope or belt in place, and there you go: The arm is unlikely to bounce and incur further injury.

But let's say you're out on a hike without any rope, and—on today of all days—you're sporting pants with an elastic waistband. Try unbuttoning a few buttons in the center of your shirt and putting your hand through the hole, or placing your hand under the strap of your backpack. A pair of pants also makes for an easy tie—just use the crotch of the jeans to support the arm, and knot the legs behind the neck. Sure, you may be the guy in the woods with your pants off, but if your arm's broken, you've got bigger problems to worry about.

16 Identify and Treat Burns

To comprehend burns and their severity, first you have to understand skin: It's the body's largest organ, and it's made up of three layers of varying thicknesses. The severity of a burn depends on how deep into these layers it penetrates, and the treatment varies for each type of burn.

FIRST DEGREE Also known as superficial burns, these minor burns can be caused by anything from hot liquids to sun exposure. They heal on their own, but it's a good idea to remove any constraining jewelry or clothing and apply a cool compress or aloe vera gel. Anti-inflammatory drugs will hasten healing.

SECOND DEGREE Flame flashes, hot metals, and boiling liquids cause this burn, which usually penetrates the skin's second layer. You'll know if you've got one because blisters will form, and it takes longer than a few days to heal. Usually it's enough to flood the site with cool water and trim away any loose skin (but leave the blisters intact to prevent infection). A daily slather of aloe vera and a nonadhesive dressing are also recommended. The exception? If the burn is larger than 3 inches (7.5 cm) in diameter, or if the burn is on the victim's face, hands, feet, groin, or bottom, it's best to go to an emergency room for care.

THIRD DEGREE This full-thickness burn is very severe. It reaches through all three layers of the skin. In the event of a third-degree burn, treat the victim for shock and transport him or her to a hospital. Skin grafts are always required for this degree of injury.

FOURTH DEGREE Another full-thickness burn, the fourth-degree burn damages structures below the skin, such as ligaments and tendons. These burns are bad news: They destroy nerves, so the victim won't feel anything. Amputation and permanent disability are likely, so your best bet is to evacuate the victim to a medical facility immediately.

17 STEP-BY-STEP
Treat for Shock

During trauma, the circulatory system diverts the body's blood supply to vital internal organs. This redistribution of oxygen can ultimately lead to shock, which is fatal if not treated properly. Pain and fear both contribute to shock, compounding the danger from the injury.

STEP ONE Recognize the symptoms of shock, such as rapid pulse, gray or pale skin (especially around the lips), and cold, clammy skin on which the sweat doesn't evaporate. Other symptoms, such as gasping for air, nausea, and vomiting, can occur as the condition worsens.

STEP TWO Have the victim lie down, keeping his or her head low. Treat any outward injuries, such as fractures or bleeding.

STEP THREE Elevate the victim's feet slightly, carefully avoiding any injuries to the legs.

STEP FOUR Loosen restrictive clothing, such as belts—it'll help the victim breathe more freely.

STEP FIVE Keep the victim warm with items such as blankets or coats.

STEP SIX Keep talking to focus the victim's mind, and reassure him or her that all will be well.

18 Sense Your Surroundings

Many people walk around with their heads stuck where the sun never shines, missing critical signs that can impact their well-being. The most basic urban survival skill is making sure you're not one of those people. Situational awareness is key to getting out of tricky scenarios—or, better yet, avoiding them entirely.

LOOK AROUND YOU When you turn a corner or enter a room, watch out for potential dangers—and possible escape routes. Observe how people are behaving, since that can clue you in to trouble spots you'll want to avoid.

LISTEN TO RUMORS Many will be false, but information from credible sources can help you decide which people or places you should probably stay away from.

SENSE DANGER Your nose can alert you to urban danger, be it fire or a gas leak. You'll likely hear a commotion before you see it. And if something looks out of place, it is. Don't investigate. Get away.

KNOW THE NUMBERS
Street Crime

8 P.M. TO 3 A.M. Time frame when most muggings occur.

25 Percent higher likelihood that you will be mugged while in London than in Harlem.

3 Number of mugging-related deaths that happen in New York City every year.

44.5 Percentage of robberies that are confrontational, such as muggings.

90 Percentage of people arrested for robbery who are male.

50 Number of children mugged daily in London, mostly for their cell phones.

5 Age of the youngest mugger on record.

91 Age of the oldest pickpocket on record.

3 Number of people commonly involved in a pickpocket operation: the blocker (obstructs), the grabber (grabs), and the shill (takes the handoff).

115,000 Number of people pickpocketed in Barcelona during a recent one-year period.

RICH SAYS

"Obvious but true: If you don't stand on a corner where drugs are sold, you're less likely to be involved in a drug-related shooting. Every town has its rough spots—stay out of 'em."

19 Foil a Pickpocket

Alertness is the best defense against light-fingered predators. Pickpockets prefer crowded places like tourist attractions and rush-hour buses where they can move in and out undetected. They often work in pairs or small groups, so be wary of diversions such as a person falling down or causing a commotion. And sure, that street musician sounds great, but he might also have a partner working the crowd. Likewise, never assume a panhandler is alone.

Avoid theft by keeping your wallet in a front pocket rather than a rear one. If a person bumps into you, immediately make sure you still have your valuables.

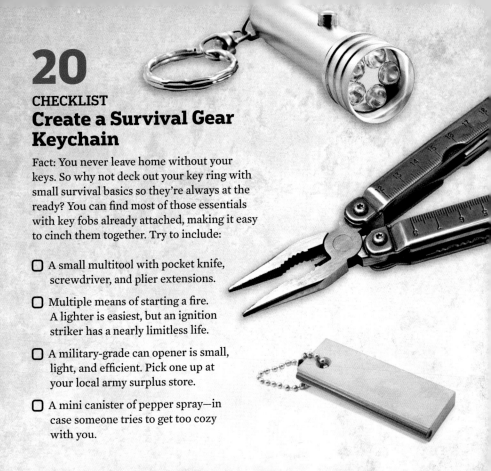

20

CHECKLIST
Create a Survival Gear Keychain

Fact: You never leave home without your keys. So why not deck out your key ring with small survival basics so they're always at the ready? You can find most of those essentials with key fobs already attached, making it easy to cinch them together. Try to include:

- [ ] A small multitool with pocket knife, screwdriver, and plier extensions.

- [ ] Multiple means of starting a fire. A lighter is easiest, but an ignition striker has a nearly limitless life.

- [ ] A military-grade can opener is small, light, and efficient. Pick one up at your local army surplus store.

- [ ] A mini canister of pepper spray—in case someone tries to get too cozy with you.

21 Drop a Decoy Wallet

Out of the darkness, some jerk approaches you with a blade or a gun and demands your money. Even if you're broke, this guy isn't going to believe you. He might decide to take you down and search your corpse. To avoid that ugly scenario, carry a drop wallet: a decoy (maybe filled with a few singles or even some play money) that you can toss on the ground as a distraction to keep your assailant busy while you run away. A caution: If you use this tactic, don't let the crook catch up with you. He'll have an attitude about your attempt to trick him.

22

Hit Where It Counts

If someone attacks you, fight back. And don't just flail around blindly—place your blows strategically for maximum impact. If you target fragile areas of your attacker's body and strike with an elbow or a closed fist, you could stun an assailant, buying yourself the time to get out of there. But use this information responsibly: Reserve the more injurious moves for fights that truly require it.

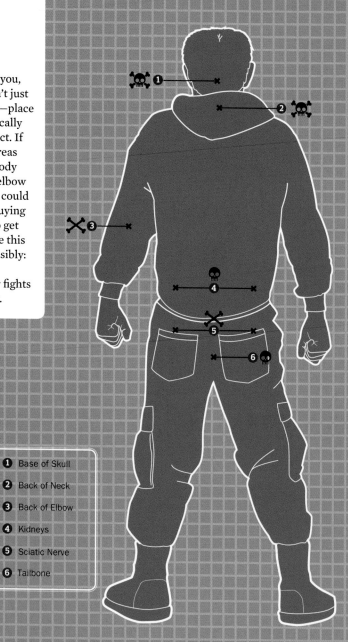

1. Base of Skull
2. Back of Neck
3. Back of Elbow
4. Kidneys
5. Sciatic Nerve
6. Tailbone

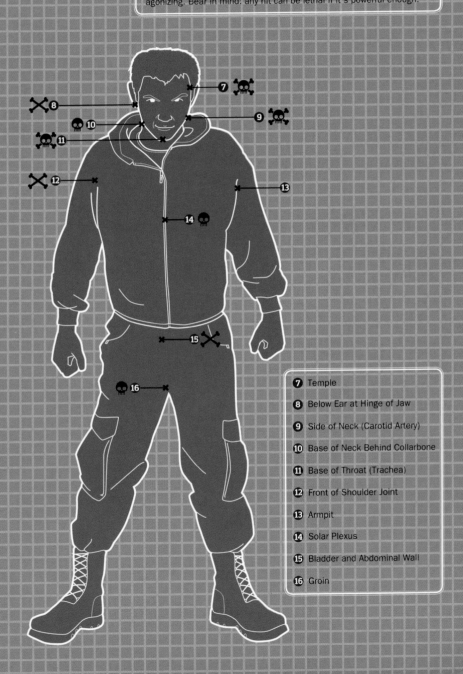

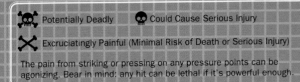
Potentially Deadly ☠ ☠ Could Cause Serious Injury

☠ Excruciatingly Painful (Minimal Risk of Death or Serious Injury)

The pain from striking or pressing on any pressure points can be agonizing. Bear in mind: any hit can be lethal if it's powerful enough.

7 Temple

8 Below Ear at Hinge of Jaw

9 Side of Neck (Carotid Artery)

10 Base of Neck Behind Collarbone

11 Base of Throat (Trachea)

12 Front of Shoulder Joint

13 Armpit

14 Solar Plexus

15 Bladder and Abdominal Wall

16 Groin

23 Defend with Pepper Spray

Pepper spray isn't made to scare someone; it's meant to disable. So only pull it out when you mean to use it, and only if you know how to use it correctly.

For starters, don't extend your shooting arm, or the assailant might grab your hand (and with it your defensive weapon, which he or she could easily turn against you). Instead, reach out your other arm and yell "Stop!" to distract your attacker. Hold the canister slightly below and in front of your chin. Aim at your assailant's face, firing a two-to-three-second burst when he or she is within range. Back up as you spray to put distance between you. This backward movement also helps keep you out of the spray zone.

24

STEP-BY-STEP

Find Pepper Spray Alternatives

A canister of wasp or hornet spray is a great stand-in for oleoresin capsicum (pepper spray). The insecticide is less expensive; it has an adjustable spray; it's available at grocery, hardware, and some convenience stores; and it effectively disables an assailant.

Or make some home-brewed pepper spray of your own:

STEP ONE Mix 2 tablespoons of cayenne pepper powder with enough rubbing alcohol to make a thin paste.

STEP TWO Add 12 drops of baby oil and mix again.

STEP THREE Strain the mixture through a fabric or paper filter. (A coffee filter will do the trick.)

STEP FOUR Pour the resulting liquid into a pump bottle with an adjustable nozzle to control the spray.

25 Make a Serious Fist

If you're not careful, you can break your own thumb when you throw a punch. Yeah, that would end the fight fast—but not the way you want. Punching with your thumb tucked inside fingers is a no-no. Instead, keep your thumb on the outside, hold your fist loosely, and strike with the knuckles of your first two fingers. Aim for these weak points:

ADAM'S APPLE Strike to knock the wind out of your attacker.

UNDERARM If an armpit is exposed, a punch there can temporarily impair the entire arm.

NOSE A good punch here can result in whiplash, bleeding, and confusion.

26 Master Basic Fighting Technique

If a stranger corners you in an alley, there's only one escape route: through your attacker. The best way to protect yourself from injury (and take out your assailant) is to disable him or her. Then get away fast—don't prolong a physical altercation any longer than what's necessary to let you escape.

PARRY You can ward off an incoming blow by thrusting it aside with your arms or legs, a move called *parrying*. Effective blocks follow a circular motion either inward or outward, depending on where the threat is coming from. Use your arms and hands to parry attacks from punches, high kicks, and weapons. Parry with your legs to deflect kicks or low strikes.

27 Clutch a Roll of Quarters

Want to pack more of a punch? Tightly grip a roll of quarters—the added weight will turn your fist into a more powerful weapon. The solid support inside your closed hand will make your fist feel as if it's made of stone, and also help prevent injury to your hand while you wail on a bad guy.

PUNCH Bring your fist to waist level, with your elbow pulled back. Step forward with the opposite foot as you punch, landing the blow as your foot hits the ground. Aim for vulnerable targets such as the nose, the throat, or the ultrasensitive solar plexus.

KICK High kicks take lots of practice and finesse, so concentrate on delivering powerful kicks to lower targets. Raise your foot to knee level and thrust the kick forward toward the gut, groin, or knee of your assailant. Step forward and follow through with punches and more kicks. Don't stop until your attacker is disabled or stunned enough for you to make a safe and fast retreat.

28 Defend Yourself with Your Keys

A parking lot can be a dangerous place, especially at ni[ght]. While walking to and from your vehicle, be ready to fe[nd] off an attack. Make a weapon by gripping your key ring in your fist with individual keys protruding between yo[ur] fingers. A slashing blow to an attacker's face (particula[rly] the eyes or throat) causes serious injury. While you're a[t] it, hit the panic button on your key ring: It'll activate yo[ur] car alarm and hopefully get you rescued.

29 Disarm an Attacker

When you're facing an armed assailant, your goal is to escape injury and, above all, to stay alive. Avoid a stare-down that might infuriate your attacker, and always submit to demands for your possessions. But if things reach a point where you have no other choice but to disarm the bad guy or die, surprise your attacker with explosive violence.

AVOID A KNIFE Stay back so your attacker can't slice you, then deploy the Nike defense: Run. If you can't escape, grab the attacker's wrist and angle the blade away.

SNATCH A CLUB Move quickly; it'll reduce your assailant's ability to swing a club. To release his grip, push him back, grab his wrist, and then twist it violently.

GRAB A GUN First, pivot out of the line of fire by turning sideways, rather than facing your attacker head-on. Then gain control of the shooter's wrist with one hand and his gun with your other. Twist the gun away from your body and down to disarm.

30

STEP-BY-STEP
Handle an Intruder

There are few things more horrifying than being confronted by a stranger who has broken into your home. Here's what to do if it happens.

STEP ONE If you hear someone trying to enter, don't investigate: Dial 911. Police recommend using a land line, as the call will be routed to local police rather than state agencies. Stay on the line—the operator will continue to hear what's going on, which can help speed up the dispatch.

STEP TWO Escape. Just about anything is better than being trapped inside with a criminal. Even if you can only make it to the backyard, you can yell for help or try to break through a fence.

STEP THREE If you are trapped, don't resist. Most home invasions are about obtaining property, which isn't as valuable as your life—ever. Give the robbers what they ask for.

STEP FOUR If you can't escape and you own a weapon, consider arming yourself. But make sure you have enough control over the situation to keep the weapon out of the home invader's hands.

31
CHECKLIST
Secure Your Home

☐ Make yourself a less appealing target. Keep valuables in secure locations—such as bank lockboxes—instead of home safes or hiding places.

☐ Don't discuss your valuables and material possessions with others.

☐ Use only licensed, reputable workers for in-home repairs, and always check ID.

☐ Install motion-activated lights on the exterior of your house. Leave on a few interior lights while you're out.

☐ Keep all windows and doors locked, including garage doors. Opt for additional locking mechanisms, such as deadbolts or locking bars for sliding-glass doors. You can also wedge a cut-off broom handle behind sliding doors and windows.

☐ Get a guard dog. Or two.

Home Invasion

ONE NIGHT, WE CAME HOME TO A HOUSE THAT SEEMED SECURE: THE DOORS WERE LOCKED, THE ALARM WAS SET, AND THE PORCH LIGHT WAS ON AS USUAL.

MY HUSBAND WENT DOWN TO INVESTIGATE. I THREW MY PEPPER SPRAY TO HIM AND STOOD ON THE LANDING, WATCHING AS HE METHODICALLY CHECKED OUT EVERY ROOM.

ALL SEEMED NORMAL UNTIL HE TURNED ON THE BACK PORCH LIGHT—HE WAS FACE-TO-FACE WITH AN INTRUDER ON THE OTHER SIDE OF THE GLASS DOOR! HE YELLED AND I DIALED 911 FROM OUR LAND LINE.

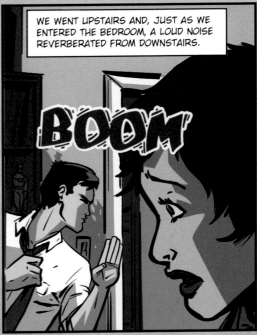

WE WENT UPSTAIRS AND, JUST AS WE ENTERED THE BEDROOM, A LOUD NOISE REVERBERATED FROM DOWNSTAIRS.

BOOM

WHITE MALE, MIDDLE 30S, SHORT BLACK HAIR, WEARING TENNIS SHOES AND A GREEN SWEATSHIRT . . .

THE WOULD-BE BURGLAR TOOK OFF. MY HUSBAND SHOUTED A DESCRIPTION, WHICH I RELAYED TO THE POLICE. SOON WE HEARD SIRENS, AND WITHIN MINUTES, THEY'D APPREHENDED A SUSPECT.

SURE ENOUGH, IT WAS THE GUY. THE COP EXPLAINED THAT OUR CALLING 911 IMMEDIATELY AND DESCRIBING—INSTEAD OF CHASING—THE INTRUDER ALLOWED THE POLICE TO CATCH HIM RAPIDLY.

32

Figure Out If Someone Is Armed

If an assailant's packing heat, you will definitely want to know about it. Look for these telltale signs:

BEWARE THE BULGE Criminals don't usually holster their weapon. It's often in their waistband or a pocket, causing an unusual bump or a weight that makes clothes hang crooked.

STUDY BODY LANGUAGE Behavior is an important tell. Tip-offs include repeatedly touching a spot where a weapon might be hidden or adjusting something that could be a gun.

TRUST YOUR SPIDEY SENSE A guy who's wearing a trench coat on a hot day may have the flu. Or he may be carrying a gun under that coat.

 DO THIS, NOT THAT
Self-Defense

DO swallow your pride to avoid a brawl. But if you can't get away, fight dirty. You're in it to injure someone and be done with it, not to score sportsmanship points with a referee. If you're fighting fairly, your strategy sucks.

DON'T raise your fists and take a stance like the Karate Kid. You're not here to put on a show, and— unless you actually *are* a black belt—all that fancy footwork could possibly make you more vulnerable to your opponent.

33 Conceal a Weapon

When choosing a weapon for concealed carry, remember that smaller is easier. If your weapon becomes visible, you'll scare people and possibly make yourself a target. In almost all cases, a permit is required to carry a concealed weapon.

KEEP IT ON YOUR HIP There's a wide range of holsters for your belt, the small of your back, and your shoulder. All of these work well—just as long as you don't remove your jacket.

STASH IT Other options include a day pack, a briefcase, or a purse. The drawbacks are relative inaccessibility and increased risk that you might lose control of your weapon.

34 CHECKLIST
Improvise a Weapon

Say you need to defend yourself, but you don't have a gun or can't get to your gun safe quickly. All is not lost, especially since your home is probably chock-full of defensive weapons.

☐ Rolling pins, pots, and pans make great clubs.

☐ Use knives and forks for a dinner to remember.

☐ Blow cayenne pepper into an attacker's eyes.

☐ The jagged edge of a broken china plate can be an effective cutting weapon.

☐ In a pinch, a broom or mop handle, a fireplace poker, or even a barrage of knickknacks can be pressed into defensive service.

☐ Wrap something heavy (such as a brick or a can of soda) in a sock or pillowcase, then swing it to strike from farther away.

35 Wield a Tactical Flashlight

A tactical flashlight is specially designed for use in combat zones, and you can pick one up at a sporting goods store near you. What's so great about it? It's two weapons in one package—which is awfully James Bond. Pretty slick, eh?

SHINE A LIGHT Grip the flashlight with your thumb on the switch button. Raise your fist and switch on the light, aiming directly into your assailant's eyes. That should temporarily blind him.

DELIVER A SMACKDOWN The second weapon is the flashlight's sharply scalloped front edge. Bring it down repeatedly with hammer blows on your attacker's nose and eyes.

36 STEP-BY-STEP
Stash Valuables in a Book

What robber is going to peruse your bookshelf, much less take down a volume and read a passage? None. So transform a book into a safe, pack it with small but valuable items, and put it on a shelf, camouflaged by the classics.

STEP ONE Pick out a hardback that blends in with your books.

STEP TWO Turn ten to twenty pages in and use a clamp to hold those pages against the front cover.

STEP THREE Use puzzle glue (it has a firm hold and dries clear) to bind the outside edge of the remaining pages. Apply a few coats, smoothing out any sloppy areas, until the pages are stuck together.

STEP FOUR Remove the clamp, then put the book in a vice or under a cinder block to keep the pages smooth as they dry. It'll take about 24 hours.

STEP FIVE Open the book, measure and mark the space you intend to cut out from the glued-together pages, and then use a razor blade to hollow them out.

37 Make a DIY Alarm

Burglars want to enter silently, burgle quietly, and then leave without a sound. That's why you want a noisy alarm system. If you don't have an in-home security system, you can achieve a similar effect with common household items.

PROTECT OUTSIDE Start in your yard, where a burglar must tread before he or she has a chance to reach your home. Outside motion sensors are commonly used to turn on lights, but up the ante by connecting a sprinkler system to the same sensors. It's one thing to illuminate a burglar; Just imagine his surprise when he's not only lit up but soaked. He's leaving fast—and he's not coming back.

WARN INSIDE Place door chimes on the backs of all interior doors. If the door moves, the bell will let you know that something's up. You can also put bells on the inside handles of doors or on window latches.

SQUEAK AND CREAK Homes often come with natural alarms, and you have the tactical advantage of knowing where the noisy spots are. Don't repair squeaky floorboards or oil your door hinges. If you know the third stair creaks when you step on it, leave it that way. These passive alarms are effective. You'll get used to the noise, but they'll grab your attention if they sound when they shouldn't. The best part? They won't cost you a dime.

Build an Outlet Safe

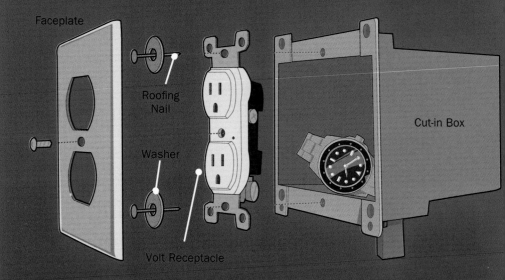

Faceplate

Roofing Nail

Washer

Volt Receptacle

Cut-in Box

Need a wall safe? Improvise one with this decoy electrical outlet—and hope burglars don't try plugging in anything.

STEP ONE Head to the hardware store and pick up a few parts: a faceplate, a residential-grade volt receptacle, a cut-in box, and some roofing nails and washers.

STEP TWO Place the cut-in box on the wall where you want your safe and trace around it. Cut the hole with a drywall saw.

STEP THREE Slide the cut-in box into the hole—this is your safe. Fill it up with small valuables.

STEP FOUR The receptacle has two holes, one at its top and one at its bottom. Slide the roofing nails through the washers and then through these holes.

STEP FIVE Attach the receptacle to the box by sliding the nails into the box's top and bottom holes.

STEP SIX Screw the faceplate onto the receptacle.

39 Avoid Identity Theft

People want to be you. They also want to use your name, credit cards, identification numbers, and bank accounts to buy things for themselves and have you pay for them. They're identity thieves—and they do business to the tune of billions of dollars a year.

To protect yourself from having your identity stolen, it helps to know how these criminals operate.

TRASH SNOOPERS They rummage through your garbage, looking for papers with credit-card, checking-account, and personal-identification numbers.

SKIMMING When processing your card at a restaurant or store, it's easy to skim your account number from your card's magnetic strip. So use cash instead.

PHISHING On the phone or online, when someone says he or she is from your bank and asks you to verify your account number, don't take the bait.

MAIL REROUTERS Criminals use a change-of-address form to divert your bills to another location so they can steal your account numbers or set up new credit cards without your knowledge.

CLASSIC THEFT They also might resort to old-fashioned robbery by stealing your wallet or purse and using the personal information in it.

To protect your identity, burn or shred all discarded papers with any account information, especially anything with government-issued identification numbers. Use an identity-theft service to track activity on your accounts and monitor your statements for charges you didn't make.

40 STEP-BY-STEP
Pick a Lock

Have to get through a locked door? Don't let the fact that you don't have the key stand in your way. It's not hard to pick a lock of the pin-and-tumbler variety—that's the kind where pairs of pins hold a cylinder in place. The trick is pushing the pins up one at a time until they're no longer blocking the cylinder's ability to rotate. When all the pins are out of the way, presto: The tumbler turns, the lock opens, and you're in.

Ideally, you'll have a tension wrench and a pick from a lock-picking tool set, but you can also use a couple of bobby pins.

STEP ONE Insert the wrench into the keyhole and determine which way the cylinder rotates to unlock. It'll give a little bit when turned the correct way. Keep applying pressure to the wrench to keep the cylinder held open that fraction of an inch.

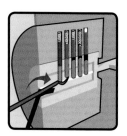

STEP TWO Insert the pick into the keyhole above the wrench, and find the pins locking the cylinder in place. Start with the farthest pin, pushing it up until you hear a click—that sound means the pin has been pushed out of the way.

STEP THREE Repeat with the rest of the pins until they've all been pushed out of the cylinder. Give the wrench a twist and *voila!*

STEP FOUR Use the wrench or bobby pin to turn the cylinder and open the lock.

41 Learn If Your Home Is Bugged

So you suspect someone is eavesdropping on you, but you can't find the bug. You could buy a bug detector, or you could just do some old-fashioned sleuthing.

CHECK THE WALLS Look behind anything hanging on the wall, like picture frames and mirrors. Scope out air vents for small cameras or microphones hidden within.

LOOK DOWN Scan for discolored carpeting or inconsistencies in the floor's finish. These could indicate that someone has replaced a section of the floor or carpet to conceal a bug underneath it.

42 Lose a Tail

You probably know the feeling: The hair stands up on the back of your neck, telling you that someone is following you. If that happens while you're on the road, you need to figure out if you're really being tailed—or if you've been reading too many detective novels.

KNOW THE SCENE Most drivers tail you from your home or office. As you enter your car, see if there are any unfamiliar vehicles nearby and notice if they leave at the same time as you.

DRIVE AS IF YOU'RE LOST In an urban setting, the easiest way to confirm if a car is really on your tail is to make four successive left turns. Someone might make one or two with you, but the chances that someone else is driving in exactly the same square are pretty small.

MIX IT UP Change lanes frequently and vary your speed, then see if the person is still following you.

MAKE A BEELINE Is the car still riding your bumper? You've got a tail all right. Your safest bet is to drive directly to a public place—ideally, a police station.

KEEP COOL You might be tempted to floor it, but you'll do better to keep calm and drive deliberately. Make sure you don't box yourself in at intersections or stoplights, and travel through well-populated areas.

FIND A SAFE SPOT Your home or office may beckon as a sanctuary, but if this person doesn't already know where you live or work, you want to keep it that way.

RICH SAYS
"Just because you're paranoid doesn't mean people aren't out to get you."

FEEL YOUR WAY Don't just rely on your eyes. Use your hands to feel along the backs of objects for hidden recording devices.

PRICK UP YOUR EARS Listen for changes in volume during phone conversations, or unexplained static in radio or television broadcasts. The transmitters of most bugs interfere with broadcast signals.

43

Beware Common Poisons

We all know it's important to keep household cleansers, detergent, and bleach away from children. The same goes for medicines: Pills can look like candy to kids. But do other dangerous substances lurk in your home?

IN THE BATHROOM Beware of nail polish remover, shampoo, and even mouthwash. In fact, due to their ingredients or alcohol content, the majority of personal-care products can be poisonous if swallowed.

IN THE GARAGE Pesticides, paints, paint thinners and removers, fuel, and oil are all dangerous to inhale or swallow. That's pretty obvious just from the smell, but other substances to watch out for are antifreeze and windshield washer fluid, which are brightly colored and may have a sweet taste and smell—but are deadly.

IN THE KITCHEN AND PANTRY It's a fairly well-known fact that raw or undercooked poultry and fish can be a source of foodborne illnesses like salmonella. Less well known is the fact that uncooked beans also warrant caution. Nearly all varieties of beans, especially red kidney beans, contain substances called lectins, which the cooking process breaks down. But if beans are eaten uncooked, they can cause nausea, vomiting, and diarrhea.

INSIDE ELECTRONICS Many household gadgets run on various batteries, from tiny button-sized ones to honking-big D-cells. Batteries contain nasty hydroxides that can be harmful if inhaled and life-threatening if swallowed.

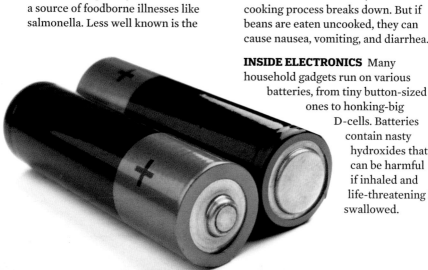

44
Save a Poisoning Victim

Helping a poisoning victim can be tricky, since there's no one-size-fits-all solution. But in every case, it's vital to find out what the toxin is and seek help.

STEP ONE Make sure the victim is breathing. If not, call 911 to summon an emergency crew.

STEP TWO Check for any remaining poisonous substance in the victim's mouth. If you find any, wipe it away.

STEP THREE If the victim isn't breathing and you've been certified in CPR, begin rescue breathing.

STEP FOUR If the toxin is a household product, check the label for advice, or contact your local poison control hotline. Do not induce vomiting unless you are instructed to do so.

STEP FIVE If the victim goes to the emergency room, take the pill bottle or package that contained what was ingested. That will help doctors start proper treatment immediately.

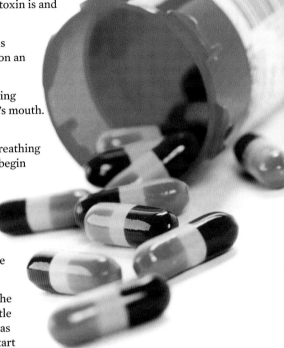

45 Soak Up Poison

Wouldn't it be swell if there were a simple pill to take after accidentally ingesting a common poison? There's no cure-all, but you might try activated charcoal. (No, not the kind of charcoal you use on your grill—this stuff's only available at pharmacies.) A mainstay in many first-aid kits, this light and practically tasteless powder binds with ingested poisons and prevents your body from absorbing them. But before taking it, check with your local poison control center, as activated charcoal could hurt—not help—if taken in combination with certain toxins.

46

Install Smoke Detectors

Trust me: If a fire ever starts in your home, you'll want to know about it. So make sure there's at least one smoke alarm in every room of your house, except for bathrooms and closets.

SAVE THE DATE Before mounting your smoke detector, write the date of purchase on the alarm. (After eight years pass, swap it out for a new one.)

HANG IT HIGH You know the old adage about smoke rising? It's true. So mount your detector on the ceiling away from windows and doors and at least 4 inches (10 cm) from the wall. Avoid placing one in the path of heat or steam coming from the kitchen or bathroom; otherwise it'll go off all the time.

MOUNT IT RIGHT All smoke detectors come with specific mounting instructions. Most make it easy for you: Installation requires little more than a screwdriver and two screws. Some types are even adhesive.

TEST IT OFTEN You should check your detector once a month to ensure that it's working properly. Simply push the button until you hear a loud noise confirming that all is as it should be. If there's no sound, you've got a dud—replace it.

KEEP BATTERIES FRESH Replace the battery once a year. If it starts making an annoying chirping sound, that's your cue that it's time for new juice.

47 Make Your Home Fire-Safe

Home fires are scary stuff, but they're largely preventable. Follow these guidelines and fret no more.

WATCH APPLIANCES Keep appliances such as toaster ovens, coffeemakers, fans, and space heaters away from water sources and flammable materials. Unplug them when they're not in use. As for water heaters, furnaces, and dryers,

clean their vents regularly and check that the ignition systems or pilot lights are operating correctly.

BEWARE THE GAS If your home runs on natural gas, check the system for loose fittings, malfunctioning pilot lights, or nearby flammable materials. If you smell even a whiff of gas, have a professional come in to check for a leak.

48 Prevent Home Electrical Fires

Crack open one of your walls and you'll find a network of powerful circuits and wires. These keep your lights on and your appliances working—and they can also send your house up in smoke if you're not careful.

WATCH THE LIGHTS If lights are flickering on and off, or if they make noise or give off a smoky odor, you've probably got faulty wiring. Call an electrician. If he or she doesn't spot a problem, you've got poltergeists—or an incompetent electrician.

VISIT YOUR FUSE BOX Every home has at least one—it's often hidden behind a panel in the basement or garage. Check for signs of trouble, like circuit breakers or fuses with multiple wires crammed into individual terminals, since those are likely to blow. While you're there, scan for signs of corrosion and smoky residue. Take a look to ensure that wires aren't precariously spliced and that the insulation around them appears to be in good shape.

PICK THE RIGHT PLUGS Try to use electrical sockets and plugs that are grounded—they provide protection against electrocution. (In the United States, look for models that have three prongs—most modern appliances do.) If your home doesn't have grounded outlets, have an electrician install them.

CHECK FOR PESTS Rodents love to gnaw on wires and cables, chewing through crucial insulation that prevents the electrical current from sparking. Every now and then, head to your attic, basement, garage, and any crawl spaces you have. Check wiring to make sure it's intact. If not, get it replaced—and call an exterminator, while you're at it.

ASSESS AND RESPOND
Fight a Fire

Not all fires start the same way, so why would they all be extinguished the same way? You should know the best tactics for fighting each class of fire (especially those that are most likely to happen in your home) and always have the correct extinguishers on hand.

TYPE OF FIRE

COMMON COMBUSTIBLES

Class A fires are the most common household fires and the easiest to extinguish. They usually involve flammable materials such as wood, paper, clothing, and some plastics.

FLAMMABLE LIQUIDS AND GASES

Another type of common household fire, class B fires spring from combustible liquids and gases such as motor oil, gasoline, or common solvents. Water can spread these fires rather than extinguish them.

ELECTRICAL

Electrical fires ignite and burn in live electrical equipment such as computers, fax machines, household appliances, and wall outlets. These are doubly dangerous, as they can also deliver a shock.

50

STEP-BY-STEP
Use a Fire Extinguisher

Looking for something to read on a quiet evening? Check out the instructions for your fire extinguisher. It's good to know how to use that thing before you're faced with an inferno, and you can call the rules to mind by remembering PASS: Pull, aim, squeeze, and sweep.

STEP ONE Pull the pin from the handle.

STEP TWO Aim the nozzle at the base of the flames, not at the flames themselves.

STEP THREE Squeeze the handle to release short bursts of spray to knock down the flames and longer pulls to fully extinguish them.

STEP FOUR Sweep side to side until the fire is out. You typically have about ten seconds of operating time before the extinguisher is empty.

RESPONSE

You can use plain old water to douse these flames. Smothering or a CO_2 extinguisher may also work in a pinch.

Spray a CO_2 extinguisher to remove crucial oxygen from the fire. You can also throw a wet blanket over the flames.

A class C CO_2 extinguisher eliminates the fire while keeping you safe from electrical current—never use water!

Use a class D extinguisher to extinguish these flames. Sodium chloride or sodium carbonate can also help, as can copper or graphite powders.

The sodium bicarbonate in a class K extinguisher will put out a kitchen fire. You can also throw baking soda on it.

51
Escape a Burning House

The key to surviving a fire in your home is having an effective plan in place before the smoldering starts.

KNOW WHERE TO GO Visibility is nearly zero in smoky conditions, so you need to know your escape route by heart. Rooms may have more than one exit, so consider which ones would work best in different situations.

STAY LOW Heat rises. So does smoke and flame. When trying to escape a burning building, get on your hands and knees and crawl toward an exit. If possible, cover your mouth and nose with a damp cloth to help reduce smoke inhalation.

ANTICIPATE Before you open a door, feel for heat on the flat surface rather than the doorknob, which could be dangerously hot. Look under the door, for visible flames. If you have any doubts, head to a secondary exit.

SHUN STAIRS If you're trapped in an upper level of a burning house, get out through a window. All exits above the first story should have escape ladders at the ready for just such an emergency. Don't use a stairway, because it can act like a chimney, funneling heat and smoke upward.

DON'T BE A HERO Under no circumstances should you remain inside to fight a blaze. If an initial flare-up, like a kitchen fire, is not immediately contained, evacuate right away. Run to a neighbor's, call 911, and let the professionals take care of putting out the flames.

52 Stock Fire Safety Gear

Want to protect your family, pets, and vital documents? Go beyond extinguishers and smoke alarms to outfit your home with these fire-safety extras.

COLLAPSIBLE FIRE-ESCAPE LADDER Home fires often fill stairwells and hallways, making the obvious escape routes unsafe. A number of manufacturers sell emergency ladders that roll up and fold to a very small size for easy storage. When you need the ladder, you can quickly unfurl it, hook it over a windowsill, and climb down to safety. Ideally, you should have a ladder in every upstairs bedroom.

FIREFIGHTER ALERT SIGNS You may be overcome by smoke or otherwise unable to communicate. Or firefighters may be rushing into your home so quickly that there's no time to get their attention. That's when stickers or signs alerting rescuers to the presence of children and pets can be lifesavers. Many fire departments give out these stickers. Or you can make your own—be sure to laminate them so they're sturdy.

FIRE SAFE Put copies of important documents and electronic files in a fireproof, waterproof safe, along with any irreplaceable sentimental items. These safes range in size from tiny to enormous.

53 Smother a Fire

Fires need three things to thrive: heat, air, and fuel. Take away any one of these and the fire goes out. An effective way to extinguish a small fire is to deny it air. Use a heavy blanket or coat to completely cover the fire, and press down forcefully. Don't toss it lightly on the flames, or it will feed the fire. If a pan on the stove ignites, smother it with a metal lid.

54 Steer with Blown Tires

BLAM! When a tire blows out, it pulls the vehicle in the direction of the flat. Fight the urge to overcorrect or to slam on the brakes, which will cause a skid. Instead, hold the steering wheel firmly, ease off the accelerator, switch on your turn signal, and start moving toward the shoulder of the road. Once there, switch on the emergency flasher to warn approaching vehicles.

55 Deal with Brake Failure

You press on the brake pedal and it goes to the floor without slowing the vehicle. Now what? Don't turn off the ignition and remove the key: The steering column will lock. Leave your foot off the accelerator to slow down and negotiate traffic and turns as best you can. If you're going downhill and picking up speed, shift to a lower gear (even automatic transmissions give you this ability) and gradually apply the emergency brake. If there's an uphill escape route, take it.

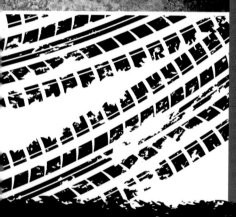

56 STEP-BY-STEP
Get Out of a Skid

The first sign of a skid may not come until you suddenly lose control and end up heading sideways down the highway. To regain control, try this:

STEP ONE Resist the temptation to hit the brakes. To steer out of the skid, you need to have the tires rolling, not locked up.

STEP TWO It may be counterintuitive, but turn the steering wheel in the direction of the skid. Do this gently, without overreacting. If your wheels start to skid in the other direction, turn the steering wheel in that direction. Be prepared to straighten the wheel as the vehicle returns to its normal trajectory.

STEP THREE Apply very light pressure on the gas pedal to help bring the vehicle back into position.

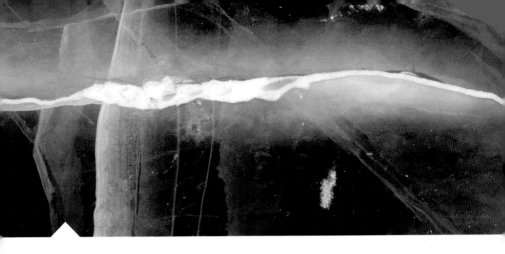

57 Drive on Black Ice

Black ice is invisible and slick as slug snot. You'll know you're driving on it because your vehicle will be totally unresponsive to steering, braking, or acceleration.

STAY HOME If you hear reports of black ice in your area, do yourself a favor and don't venture outside.

GO WITH THE FLOW Black ice basically transforms your vehicle into a sled, so all you can do is keep your foot off the brake and steer in the direction of the skid.

BUCKLE UP Wear a seatbelt—you'll likely need it.

58

Stop Hydroplaning

When tires encounter more water than the tread grooves can dissipate, the tire essentially floats on a layer of water. That's hydroplaning—and it ain't good.

READ THE CLUES When hydroplaning, the engine's revolutions per minute (RPM) sharply rises and the wheels have no traction.

EASE UP Don't turn the wheel or hit the brakes, since both will cause a skid. Instead, hold your course and ease off the accelerator, allowing your vehicle to slow down and the tires to penetrate the water layer.

59 Live Through a Cliffhanger

A car veers toward a cliff, then stops, leaving the front of the vehicle hanging in space. Way cool in a movie, supremely uncool in real life. If you find yourself hanging, what you do next can mean the difference between life and death.

CALL IN THE CAVALRY Call 911, explain your sticky situation, and give your location. If the car seems too unstable for you to safely get out of it, remain incredibly still while you wait for the rescue team.

RESCUE YOURSELF If waiting for rescue seems unwise, move very slowly to prevent unbalancing the car. Crawl into the back seat and exit through a rear door or window. If the car starts to teeter, stop and wait for someone to anchor it before you exit.

WORK TOGETHER But what if you're not alone in this car on a precipitous cliff? Those sitting in the front should move slowly to the back seat in order to keep the car's weight off the front axle. Next, exit using both sides of the car as quickly as is safe, turning to help others once outside the vehicle.

60

STEP-BY-STEP
Survive Crashing into the Water

Escaping a car that has gone underwater takes a cool head. If you panic, you probably aren't going to survive.

STEP ONE Get your seatbelt off and try to open the door before the water level gets above a few inches.

STEP TWO If that doesn't work, open the window and climb out before the water level reaches the glass. If you can't open the window, use a blunt object to break the glass so you can crawl out.

STEP THREE No go? Stay calm—though of course that's easier said than done. Wait until the car fills with water, and then try the door again. It will probably open once the water pressure inside equals the pressure outside.

61

Put Out a
Car Fire

Burning cars don't generally explode as spectacularly as they do in the movies—which is some comfort if you have to deal with one.

BE PREPARED Carry a small CO2 extinguisher in your car. If fire breaks out, it'll likely be in the engine. As soon as you smell fire, exit the car immediately. Unlatch the hood but don't fully open it. Then insert the extinguisher's nozzle into the gap and empty the extinguisher.

BE A HERO If someone else's car is burning, call 911. Pulling someone from a car should be an absolute last resort, but if you must stage a rescue, move him or her at least 100 feet (30 m) away.

62
Pack a Lifesaver
in Your Car

After a wreck, you might have trouble escaping your vehicle. The seatbelt latch might not release, doors may be damaged, or power windows may no longer operate. What you need is a tool that gets you the heck out of there. Next time you're at an auto supply store, look for a gizmo with a hooked blade on one end—perfect for cutting seatbelts— and a tip designed to break glass on the other end. Stow it in your center console so it's available if needed.

63 Avoid a Carjacking

Most carjackers are only after your car, but sometimes they want it so badly that they're willing to kill you for it. It's best to arm yourself with some preventative measures.

SIT TIGHT Keep your doors locked and your windows rolled up to deter carjackers.

LEAVE ROOM TO MANEUVER Don't box yourself in at intersections or in traffic jams.

GIVE IN FAST . . . If a carjacker confronts you, sacrifice your vehicle—it could save your life. Get out of the car and run away immediately.

. . . OR MAKE A GETAWAY Tromp on the accelerator and speed away. If you're caught in traffic, bend a few fenders if you must!

64 Play It Safe in a Parking Garage

Is there any location creepier than an empty parking garage? To cut the risk of falling victim to the robberies and attacks that go down in these spots, think about ways to protect yourself before danger materializes.

PARK WISELY Only park in well-lit areas, and avoid the top parking floor, which tends to be empty—leaving you more isolated. Park close to store entrances, exits, and security stations.

SCAN THE SCENE Be aware of your surroundings as you look for a parking place and when you're returning to your car. Look for suspicious vehicles or people loitering near your parking space.

RAISE A RUCKUS If you sense trouble but don't see anyone, activate your car alarm, wait a minute, and then get into the car and lock the doors.

ERR ON THE SIDE OF CAUTION If you spot a suspicious character as you return to your car, go back inside the store and request that someone escort you.

65 Signal from a Car Trunk

You've been abducted and locked in a car's trunk in the dead of night. You're totally helpless, right? Wrong. You can use the taillights to draw attention to your plight. To gain access to them, you might have to remove or break through a lightweight panel covering the back of the lights. Pull the wiring to make the lights go out, which will attract police interest, or cut any of the wires in two and strip back the insulation. Then touch the ends of the wires together to create short and long flashes that spell out *SOS*.

66 Escape from a Car Trunk

Trapped in a trunk? Looks like you're just gonna have to rescue yourself.

PULL THE TRUNK RELEASE If you're lucky, there will be a glow-in-the-dark T-handle trunk release. If not, look for the cable leading to the trunk release in the driver's compartment and tug it toward the front of the car. This cable is usually along the floor on the driver's side.

USE SOME TOOLS Look for a screwdriver or tire iron you can use to pry the trunk latch open. Or you can use the tire jack to pry up a corner of the trunk lid, then signal other drivers for help.

KICK YOUR WAY OUT If the car's parked and empty, kick through the backseat and crawl out through the passenger compartment to exit the vehicle.

67 Outsmart Your Kidnappers

Being kidnapped is scary stuff for sure, and I hope it never happens to you (or me). But if you should someday find yourself nabbed and stuffed in a dark closet, you should try to play your captors to your advantage.

KNOW YOUR ENEMIES Keep track of how many captors you have, noting their names, physical appearance, mannerisms, and where they fall in the hierarchy, if you detect one.

MAKE A CONNECTION Try to establish a rapport. Yes, they're kidnappers, but they probably have a human side (even Hitler liked animals). Try to get your captors to see your human side as well. You're better off if they view you as a person.

WATCH THE CLOCK Memorize your kidnappers' schedules and keep track of the passage of time. Don't have a room with a view? Pay attention to changes in temperature at dawn and dusk, bustle or quiet in the hallways, and your handlers' alertness. If it seems as if they need coffee, it just might be morning.

BE A GOOD "GUEST" This is one situation in which you have every reason to scream, shout, and kick anyone that comes near you. But don't. Follow all orders and instructions and, once you've achieved a basic rapport, try asking for any needed items, such as medicine, food, or water. Make requests in a reasonable, low-key manner.

ESTABLISH YOUR OWN ROUTINE Every day, try to do some mental as well as physical exercise—you want to be feeling clear-headed and fit when the chance for escape arises. If you can't move much, use isometric and flexing exercises to keep your muscles toned. Unless you think you're being drugged, eat what your captors give you—malnourishment makes you weak. And for mental stress, use meditation techniques to keep yourself sane.

REACH OUT Listen carefully for evidence of any other prisoners near you. If you detect the slightest sign that you're not alone, attempt communication. You may find a buddy who can help you bust out.

LOOK FOR OPPORTUNITIES Keep an eye out for patterns of behavior that you can use to your advantage. If your captors take regular smoke breaks or leave you unguarded to watch news coverage, you might have just enough time to make your escape.

68

STEP-BY-STEP
Free Yourself from Ropes

If your hands are tied and you don't have a knife (and what self-respecting kidnapper is going to let you have a knife?), you'll need to pull a Houdini to escape. Try these tactics:

STEP ONE Begin by pushing and twisting the rope or cord to see if you can reduce some of the tension in the rope.

STEP TWO Grab the lines on both sides of the knot and push them together to loosen the knot.

STEP THREE Move your arms up and down to loosen the knot even more.

STEP FOUR With persistence and luck, the knot will unravel. Congratulate yourself. You're free!

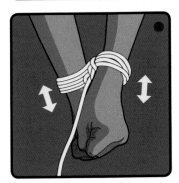

69

Deduce Where You're Being Held

A hood is thrown over your head and you're dragged into a vehicle by unknown assailants. You're powerless at the moment, but if you can figure out where you're being taken, maybe later on you can get a message to rescuers so they know where to look.

Try to estimate the time between turns and stops. How many lefts, how many rights? How many stops at intersections? Does it suddenly get darker, then bright again, as if you're going through a tunnel? What do you smell: a farm, the docks, a bakery? What do you hear: children, a train, the splash of water? What do you feel: Is the road bumpy, hilly, or crisscrossed by railroad tracks? Memorize all of this and try to put the pieces together.

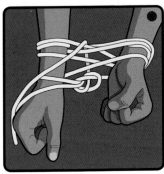

70
CASE STUDY: NABBED BY THE CARTEL
Survive an Abduction

On November 15, 1992, fishing guide Kjell von Sneidern and an Italian friend drove the remote roads along the Orinoco River borderlands between Venezuela and Colombia. The two men were en route to survey a remote location for a fishing lodge specializing in trophy payara, also known as vampire fish. Visions of toothy monsters filled their heads, but when they rounded a bend, they faced a very different kind of danger.

Recently felled trees blocked their path, and they were pulled from the vehicle at gunpoint. Surrounding them was a group of twenty young men, drug dealers who had splintered off from the more disciplined cartels. They took the two men into the jungle and demanded a $500,000 ransom.

For 72 days, the men were held captive. They were forced to travel mostly at night to avoid detection. When resting, the captors would confine von Sneidern and his companion to hammocks, littering the ground beneath them with dry sticks and leaves that acted as an alarm system. One of the captors carried a human skull with a bullet hole in it as a warning against trying to escape.

Nature also worked to confound any attempt to escape. One spring they frequented was home to a 23-foot (7- m) anaconda, and the jungle was full of other predators, including jaguars.

The two men endeavored to stay safe in their perilous captivity, safeguarding themselves against disease by taking steps like purifying drinking water. All the while, they tried to gain the good will of their captors. They were always cooperative, and gave their enemies their possessions as a means of winning them over.

Local officials were indecisive about the best way to respond, but von Sneidern's family sprang into action. They flew to the area, where they worked with officials and hired mercenaries to follow the kidnappers and rescue the two hostages.

Knowing they were being tracked, the kidnappers became desperate, and many deserted. One night, those that remained commandeered a boat and made for the Venezuelan side of the river. But the boat's motor gave out and they drifted to shore. Waiting for them were Venezuelan authorities, while von Sneidern's family and their hired guns stood guard on the Colombian side of the river. When shooting broke out, von Sneidern and his friend jumped ship, making a break for it. Moments later, a helicopter rescued the two men.

POST ASSESSMENT
Nabbed by the Cartel

Enterprising fishermen set out to find their fortune along the Orinoco River. Instead, they were kidnapped by vicious drug dealers armed to the teeth with AK-47s. Here's how they fared on our survival-o-meter.

✔ Worried about disease and out of water purification tablets, von Sneidern put two aspirin in every bottle of water they drank, which may have helped stave off dysentery.

At every opportunity, von Sneidern took off his shoes and socks to dry his feet and keep fungus from setting in—a real risk in a jungle climate.

He learned which of his captors would be most likely to be sympathetic, and he waited until they were on guard duty to ask for food or water.

He fought the urge to panic, instead remaining calm and having faith that help would come.

He gave his comb and other small personal items to some of his captors in return for kinder treatment and possible help escaping.

When von Sneidern finally got an opportunity to flee his captors, he did so decisively.

 The two men planned on setting up a tourist lodge in an area that was dangerous and too remote for immediate assistance.

They ignored the Colombian government, which was not supportive of the idea.

Neither man had a radio to call for help.

Von Sneidern's family hired mercenaries, which was successful in this case, but is generally considered a risky endeavor at best. It's better to try to work things out through your embassy.

The men were in unfamiliar territory, which made escaping their captors—who were intimately familiar with the terrain—nearly impossible.

71 Live Through a Hostage-Taking

If you're taken hostage, don't just sit there and quake. There are things you can do to improve your odds of surviving—and help the authorities foil the bad guys.

SECRETLY REACH OUT Dial emergency services (if you can do so without being detected), and leave the line open so authorities can listen in. Some stores and banks even have an emergency button—if you know where it is, push it.

DON'T ROCK THE BOAT Hostage-takers want to maintain a position of power and control. If you threaten that role, you put yourself at risk. So don't try to fight or run away (unless you feel very confident of your chances of escape). Sit where and how the hostage-takers tell you, and do exactly as they say.

BE A GOOD WITNESS You're scared for sure, but that doesn't mean you shouldn't pay attention. Your insight into the situation will be invaluable to law enforcement officials upon your release. Do your best to memorize detailed descriptions of the kidnappers (including how many there are). If you're released before other hostages, take mental notes so you can describe where the remaining hostages are being kept.

ASSESS AND RESPOND
Take a Blow

If you're being threatened, the best thing to do is get away. If that's not possible, fight back with all you've got. But the problem with fighting is that it's a two-way street— you'll get your licks in, but you may have to take some as well. Here's how.

PUNCH

If you can't avoid a punch, brace yourself. For a blow to the head, clench your jaw and move toward the attacker to lessen the extension of his arm and the power gained by the momentum. Or duck to take the blow on your forehead instead of the more breakable parts of your face. For blows to the gut, flex abdominal muscles and exhale sharply to prevent the wind from being knocked out of you.

CLUB

Being struck by a pipe or club is similar to being punched, but with a much harder object. Your first defense is to close the distance between yourself and the assailant. Try to take the blow in soft spots like large muscle masses on the thigh, which will bruise, and not directly to bones, which could shatter.

CAR IMPACT

If someone is running you down, try to get out of the direct path of the vehicle, putting heavy, stationary objects like telephone poles between you and the car. The most common car-versus-pedestrian injury is a leg break below the knee. So if you're about to be struck, roll into the impact, letting it take your weight off your feet—it's far preferable to being thrown into the car's path. Aim to land on the center of the hood and let your body roll through the impact up and over the windshield and roof.

KNIFE

Most lethal knife attacks take place inside a critical distance about two-thirds the length of the attacker's arm. The most common attack is a slash at the outer edge of this distance. Do not try to close the distance on a knife-wielding attacker. Instead, fight outside the critical distance. Try to move your body in the same direction as the slash to minimize resistance. Immediately reestablish yourself outside critical distance to avoid being cut with a return slash.

BULLET

When shooting starts, act fast. If you're against a wall, move away from it, since bullets tend to ricochet and travel along large, hard surfaces. Most lethal shots are to the head, neck, and back, so be sure to protect those sensitive zones. Turn your body to face your attacker, then drop to the floor with your legs together and your knees drawn up to protect your torso. Place your arms together in front of your head, resting your palms on top.

73 Know Basic Maritime Laws

One way to recognize when something's fishy at sea is by knowing maritime navigation and communication norms. A vessel that's ignoring these commonly understood conventions may be in trouble, or up to no good.

KNOW YOUR PLACE When two boats approach each other, one is considered privileged and the other is identified as burdened. The privileged boat has the right of way, and the burdened boat is responsible for moving out of its path. Generally, sailing vessels are privileged over motorboats. And a boat overtaking a slower vessel from the rear is burdened to that vessel.

PASS POLITELY If two vessels are coming toward each other head on, each boat should pass on the right, as they would on an American roadway. If two boats are approaching port-to-port or starboard-to-starboard, then each vessel should simply hold its course until they're safely past each other.

BE SIGNAL SAVVY Use your horn to indicate your direction. One short blast means you intend to pass on the starboard; two short blasts indicate a pass to port. Short, rapid blasts indicate imminent danger, so be prepared to take evasive action if necessary when you hear these.

74 Safeguard Against Pirates

I'll be the first to admit, they're jolly good fun in the movies: all yo-ho-ho and a bottle of rum. But real-life pirates are a serious, and sometimes deadly, threat.

STEER AWAY FROM TROUBLE Consult one of the Web sites that help recreational and commercial boaters track—and avoid—piracy hot spots.

TAKE PRECAUTIONS AT SEA If you must travel in a dangerous area, go in a convoy. At night, run without lights. Avoid using the radio and use radar to track the boats around you.

STAY SAFE ON LAND At anchor, secure all hatches with iron bars, lockable from inside.

75 Send Out a Distress Signal

If your boat is boarded by pirates, immediately lock yourself in the cabin and try to alert the authorities and other boats in the area to your plight. Use lights, foghorns, a loud-hailer, a siren, and whatever else you have at hand, and place a call for help on your radio. In case the pirates manage to swipe or disable the main radio, always conceal a small handheld Very High Frequency (VHF) marine band or ham radio below deck or in the cabin where the bad guys aren't likely to find it. Other good ways to attract attention include sending up aerial flares and putting dye markers in the water.

76

Repel Boarders from Your Boat

Be sure before taking extreme measures: You don't want to mistake an innocent fisherman who is approaching your boat seeking water for a bloodthirsty pirate with foul intent. If you're positive that you're dealing with bona fide scourges of the sea, choose your weapon wisely. Many countries prohibit firearms aboard vessels, but there are no restrictions on flare guns. And at close range, a flare gun can deliver a belly full of fire to a would-be invader. Adapters are available to allow a standard flare gun to fire .38-caliber or 12-gauge shotshell ammunition, but tests suggest these guns don't hold up well when delivering multiple rounds, so make your first shot count.

Before you decide to come out with guns blazing, you might want to consider that these guys might be armed with automatic rifles. Preserving your life and those of others on board should be your priority, even if it costs you your boat.

One Mean Machete

A GROUP OF US WERE TRAVELING THROUGH GHANA, AND WE DID OUR BEST TO BLEND IN. BUT WITH HER WESTERN ATTIRE AND MANNERISMS, WENDY STOOD OUT.

SHE KEPT FALLING BEHIND, DESPITE OUR REMINDERS TO STAY CLOSE.

I NOTICED A FEW MEN WATCHING HER WHILE SHE CHATTED WITH SOME VENDORS. I DIDN'T LIKE THE WAY THEY WERE LOOKING AT HER, SO I HEADED BACK TO ENCOURAGE HER TO MOVE ON.

AS I NEARED HER, THE MEN MADE THEIR MOVE. THEY GRABBED HER AND TRIED TO PULL HER AWAY INTO AN ALLEY.

SHE MANAGED TO BREAK FREE, AND HER ATTACKERS TURNED THEIR FOCUS ON ME. ONE OF THEM PULLED OUT A MACHETE.

HE SWUNG THE MACHETE IN A VICIOUS UPPERCUT. I DID MY BEST TO DIVE BACK OUT OF THE WAY, BUT IT HIT ME IN THE CHIN...

THE BLADE BROKE OFF IN MY JAW AS I TWISTED AWAY!

AS I COLLAPSED, I FELT THE HANDS OF PEOPLE IN MY GROUP GRAB ME AND PULL ME OUT OF THE FIGHT.

AS WE HUSTLED OUT OF THE MARKET TOWARD THE HOSPITAL, I HELD MY CHIN WHERE THE BLADE HAD BROKEN OFF.

WE WERE LUCKY TO GET AWAY.

I WANTED A GENUINE SOUVENIR OF MY AFRICAN TRIP. I DIDN'T REALIZE JUST HOW AUTHENTIC A SCAR WOULD BE.

77

Get to Know the Customs

Knowing a culture's traditions will help you maintain a lower profile while visiting or working there.

DO RESEARCH It's your job to know the dangers and sensitivities of your host nation. For example, certain hand gestures common in your own country might be rude, and some countries have gender-specific dress codes.

PICK A GOOD DAY For instance, recent protests in the Middle East have been most intense after Friday prayers. So keep a lower profile at particularly fraught times.

WATCH THE CLOCK Violence often leads to curfews. Know what they are—and adhere to them.

 DO THIS, NOT THAT
Bribes

DO be honest and direct in dealing with any person in authority. Giving respect and being courteous is more likely to get you out of a situation than aggressive confrontation.

DON'T pay bribes, even if they're demanded. You're only trading one problem for another, because if the officials turn the tables and charge you with offering a bribe, you've got a new problem that's worse than your original one.

78

Hide Money in Your Clothes

To protect your cash while traveling, conceal it on your person in places a mugger won't think of.

GET CREATIVE Money belts and hiding currency inside shoes or bras are old and expected tricks. Leg pouches concealed beneath pants or skirts are better.

HIDE A POCKET Create secret pockets inside your clothing by slitting open the hem or waist seam of your pants or the collar of your shirt. Then slip bills inside the hidden pocket.

TRAVEL LIGHT Don't stuff your secret hiding places so full of goodies that they become obvious.

79

Use the Buddy System

When traveling in unknown or unfriendly territory, there is indeed safety in numbers. The buddy system works great—but only if you have the right buddy. A sound travel companion provides a voice of reason when in doubt. Two heads are often better than one, especially in a foreign country.

Divide up responsibilities. In airport terminals, hotel lobbies, or taxi stands, make sure one person is always with your luggage. If a stranger approaches, only one person should engage, allowing the other to keep an eye out for petty thieves or pickpockets.

80 Avoid Counterfeit Cops

While doing what a police officer asks is often wise, it can make you susceptible to travel scams.

CHECK CREDENTIALS When you're in a foreign country, know who the authorities are and what uniforms they wear. Be especially wary of individuals claiming that they need to inspect your belongings.

GO TO THE STATION If a police officer asks to search your purse or wallet, politely comply—at a police station. There's no crime in asking an officer to escort you to a proper station house, so don't be bashful about asking.

81 CHECKLIST
Be a Smart Traveler

I don't want to be a buzzkill, but vacations don't mean a holiday from vigilance. Follow these guidelines for happy, crime-free travels.

☐ Check with appropriate government agencies for international travel advisories. If a place is deemed unsafe, don't go there.

☐ Be aware of the host country's entry requirements prior to travel. For instance, some require a passport be valid at least six months prior to entry. Know customs laws for both entry and reentry.

☐ Before your departure, make copies of all important documents and keep them in multiple locations in case of an emergency.

☐ Have an itinerary and share it with a trusted friend. Set check-in times. And if your itinerary changes, alert him or her immediately.

☐ Know the contact information for embassies in any country on your itinerary. Program local emergency numbers into your phone.

☐ No matter where you're staying, don't open the door without using the peephole to see who's there—just as you would if you were at home. Don't allow strangers into your room, no matter where you are.

☐ Don't display your room keys in public—you don't want strangers knowing your room number or even where you're staying.

☐ Don't carry large quantities of cash or expensive jewelry, and don't keep all your valuables or currency together in one place. Any valuables you absolutely have to bring along should be stored in the hotel or room safe deposit box, if possible.

☐ Report any suspicious persons or activities to hotel management.

☐ If you're traveling off the grid, invest in a trustworthy travel guide.

RICH SAYS
"Carry whatever emergency gear your mode of travel will permit. Always keep escape routes in mind. To minimize the target on your back, leave your bling at home."

82 Blend In for Safety

Tourists are crime targets because they often carry valuables such as passports, credit cards, and lots of cash—and they're easy to spot. While you may not conform completely with the locals, you certainly can apply some cultural camouflage to blend in.

CLOTHES Don't wear things that are easily identifiable with your own culture. For instance, if you're American, avoid wearing fanny packs, baseball caps, tennis shoes, and casual clothing with prominent brand names. Instead, dress a little nicer than you might usually, and wear colors that correspond to those worn by the majority of the host population, like bright colors in the Caribbean and muted tones in London.

FOOD You're visiting for a reason, so don't seek out your usual comfort foods while you're traveling. Unless you have to worry about foodborne illnesses, eat what the locals are eating, and try to use your utensils the way they do. Also avoid asking for common Western condiments, such as ketchup. Go with whatever ones you are given, and eat your food in the order in which it arrives. You'll not only blend in—you'll have a culinary adventure.

HABITS Most locals don't walk around reading a map, so try to figure out where you're going ahead of time. And while you're bound to take pictures in a foreign country, stow your camera in a pocket or bag rather than on a strap around your neck. Keep your voice low to avoid drawing attention to yourself.

83

STEP-BY-STEP
Exit a Tunnel Safely

Getting stuck on the subway is not only a drag—
it can also be dangerous, especially if you need to
make your own way out of the tunnel.

STEP ONE Avoid the two most dangerous
things in a subway tunnel: moving trains and
the electricity that keeps them going. Don't
walk on the tracks, because a train can come
without warning. And stay away from the third
rail—which is usually elevated and to the side of
the tracks—since it can electrocute you. Instead,
walk along the ledge adjacent to the tracks.

STEP TWO Find the emergency exits, which are
positioned along the wall and well marked.

STEP THREE Follow the signs up the stairs—
you'll likely find a dead-end metal hatch. If you
push hard against the iron bar, the hatch will
open and you can climb out onto the sidewalk
above the subway.

KNOW THE NUMBERS
Mass Transit

13 Number of people killed in the
1995 sarin gas attacks on the Tokyo
subway.

660 FEET (201 M) Plunge of the
worst cable car disaster in history,
which happened in Italy in 1976.

4 Number of suicide bombers who
carried out the London attacks in
2005, which killed 52 people and
injured more than 700.

1 in 94,242 Odds of dying in a bus
accident.

10.2 BILLION Number of public
transportation trips taken in the
United States in 2010.

355 Number of people killed in the
United States each year at railway
crossings.

13 Number of improvised explosive
devices placed on trains in the 2004
Madrid attack.

1 Person killed on the New York
subway system by a lunatic wielding a
power saw.

84 Stay Safe on Mass Transit

In general, public transit is a good thing: It gets people around fast and cheaply. But bad guys may be riding with you. Here's how to stay safe.

CHECK THE SCHEDULE Know when your train or bus is scheduled to come. Arrive close to departure, cutting down on the time you spend lingering around stops or stations. This goes triple for night rides.

AVOID DODGY STOPS Sometimes the closest station isn't the safest one. If it's poorly lit, poorly staffed, or a gathering spot for thugs, walk to a farther, safer transit hub.

SIT UP FRONT The closer you are to the driver, the more likely you are to benefit from his or her protection. Taking a seat in the back will put you out of the driver's line of vision and make you more vulnerable to mischief.

STASH GADGETS Most robberies today involve smartphones or MP3 players. Keep yours safely out of sight.

85 Survive a Human Stampede

People react differently to panic. Some stand still and make their undies wet (or worse). Others take off running and hollering as if their hair is on fire. If you find yourself in a panicked crowd, you're at risk of getting trampled. So act fast.

FIND SOME PROTECTION Look for something substantial and immovable to hide behind: a large tree, a utility pole, a structural pillar, a wall, or a vehicle. Unless the mob is in full car-rollover-and-burn mode, you might want to try

taking refuge inside a vehicle until the masses have passed.

GO WITH THE FLOW If you get trapped inside the stampede, stay on your feet and conserve your energy (don't resist the movement). Keep your arms and hands near your chest so you can create a little space around you. Try to work your way diagonally toward the edge of the crowd. You'll be out of the worst of it and more likely to find a refuge or an escape route.

Be Alert to the Risk of Terrorism

You're waiting in the airport security line and you spot an unattended bag, or a person in street clothes ducking into an area marked "Authorized personnel only." Are those danger signs? You bet—and in today's tense times, we all need to watch out for them. Report anything that strikes you as strange to authorities.

GET PARANOID As you enter a space, look for things that don't belong. Such things might include a cake box sitting on a park bench, a car that's been parked outside the mall for three days straight, or someone wearing clothing that's inappropriate for the location or time of year. (Ski masks are fine on the slopes, but creepy anywhere else.)

BEWARE PHOTOGRAPHERS Mostly people you see photographing or videotaping in a train station or airport are just tourists—but sometimes they're terrorists surveying an area so they can later commit an atrocity. Even someone sketching a metro stop may be cause for concern.

WATCH FOR LINGERERS There's a big difference between waiting for a friend and waiting to activate a bomb, though the two activities may look alike. If someone has been hanging out in an area for a long time, he or she may be up to no good—likewise if someone keeps driving or walking by an area.

CHECK THE TIME Most terrorist activity goes down during periods of high traffic. (Sadly, that's to maximize casualties.) It's easy to miss things in all the bustle, but try to keep your eyes wide open during rush hour.

GET THE DETAILS When you're reporting a dubious character or a disconcerting oddity to security personnel or the police, be as specific as you can. Relay what the person involved looked like, how he or she was dressed and behaving, and when and exactly where you spotted them. If a vehicle is involved, note the make, color, and if possible, the license plate number.

87 Prevail in a Riot

Be it political unrest or violence over a soccer match, rioting is bad news. It doesn't matter if you're home or abroad—it's wise to plan for the possibility of things getting rough. Here are some tips that'll keep you safe even if the crowd turns ugly.

KNOW WHERE YOU ARE Understand the political climate and perils in any region in which you're traveling, and pay attention to the local news every day. Similarly, keep big sporting events on your radar, as fan frenzy mixed with alcohol tends to create volatility—even for nonfans.

GET OUT OF THE CROWD Riots typically occur in streets, parking lots, and town centers. So if trouble is brewing, avoid those hot spots. Find shelter and don't go back out to watch the riot. As the bricks, bottles, rubber bullets, and tear gas canisters begin to fly, spectators may be injured—either by a rampaging mob or by those trying to restore order.

MOVE OUT If you do find yourself at the hub of it all, try to look inconspicuous and move steadily and deliberately out of the center of activity, staying close to walls to minimize exposure. The more time spent in the center of a riot, the greater the chance for injury. Your best bet is finding a place where you can hole up safely until you're certain the danger has ended.

KEEP YOUR COOL Being caught up in an unsettled mob can get you riled up, but don't let yourself be ruled by an adrenaline rush. Think rationally, pursue safety, and act as an individual, not as a member of the crowd. During riots, both authorities and rioters tend to act en masse, so chances are you'll have to rescue yourself instead of relying on others to assist you.

STEER CLEAR OF COPS The police might use riot control agents like tear gas and pepper spray. Also bear in mind that running toward police, even when you're seeking security, can be seen as threatening.

88

Know the Weapons of a Mob

Suppose you find yourself in the middle of an riot. As you make your way out of the mob, it's a good idea to have an understanding of the kinds of crowd-control weapons law enforcement agencies might use—as well as the hazards you might face from rioters.

BATONS Keep your head down and your neck covered as you move low to the ground to get yourself out of the way.

SHIELDS When the police are using their shoulders and shields to shove rioters to the side, don't resist or push back. You can lose your balance, putting yourself at risk of being trampled.

CONCUSSION GRENADES These explosives are meant to scare people, and they work! You won't be able to avoid being stunned, so hunker in place and cover your head. Use the mayhem to your advantage by darting through breaks in the crowds to safety.

WATER CANNONS Don't stand up, as you'll easily be knocked off your feet. Instead, hunch down to protect vital organs, and keep your back to the cannon as much as possible.

RUBBER BULLETS They may be less than lethal, but they sure do smart. Crouch in a ball and cover your face with your arms. Don't turn your back to the shooter, as hits to the spine can temporarily paralyze.

ROCKS AND BRICKS Being hit in the back of the head is the biggest threat from the go-to missiles of the angry masses. Duck and cover yourself as you scramble to safety.

BOTTLES A missile that shatters is especially dangerous. If bottles start flying, keep your head low with your hands shielding your eyes. Don't run through broken glass—if you trip and fall, it could cut you up.

MOLOTOV COCKTAILS The worst hazard is burning fuel splashing off pavements and onto you. Run perpendicular to the cocktail's trajectory to avoid the flames.

TEAR GAS CANISTERS Yes, the cops may have lobbed them in, but the rioters may lob them back, even if they are already discharging their nasty, harmful contents.

89

Deal with Tear Gas

Don't let the movies fool you: Wearing a wet bandanna over your face is not going to protect you from tear gas. This stuff doesn't just affect your breathing—it also coats the skin and irritates the eyes. If you get sprayed, leave the area as quickly as possible, and breathe in short bursts through your nose. Avoid rubbing your skin or eyes, which can cause chemical burns. Once out of the fray, wash the tear gas off and pour milk in your eyes if they're still irritated.

90 Evade IEDs

Civilians have no business in combat zones, but in some countries, it's quite possible that you'll unwittingly wind up in the thick of things. Modern battlefields don't always rely on modern weaponry. In fact, most rebellions rely on low-tech weapons like improvised explosive devices (IEDs).

LOOK FOR TROUBLE If you must travel down a road where IEDs may be hidden, keep a sharp eye out for things that seem out of place. Piles of rubble close to the road's edge could indicate a concealed explosive. Watch for people loitering, since most IEDs require line-of-sight triggering. Don't drive a vehicle that stands out as foreign and, if you can, hire local drivers.

DON'T LINGER Make your way through a suspicious area deliberately yet quickly—and don't stop unless you absolutely must.

91 Escape a Dirty Bomb

Perhaps the scariest terrorist threat of all is the dirty bomb: an explosive device containing radioactive material. Dirty bombs do damage not through their blast, but through the radiation that spreads afterward. Lethality depends on many factors, so authorities will broadcast the risks and let you know if you're within the evacuation zone.

If authorities warn of the presence of radiation, immediately cover your nose and mouth with your hand or a cloth, and take shelter in an undamaged building. Close all windows and doors, and turn off heaters, air conditioners, or any other ventilation systems. If you suspect exposure to radiation, remove your clothing and, if possible, wash it or find something else to wear. Monitor emergency broadcasts for instructions on how and where you should proceed.

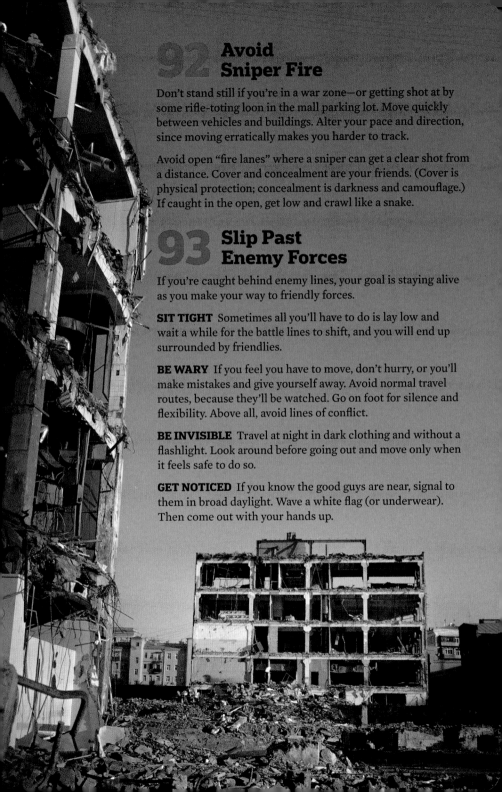

92 Avoid Sniper Fire

Don't stand still if you're in a war zone—or getting shot at by some rifle-toting loon in the mall parking lot. Move quickly between vehicles and buildings. Alter your pace and direction, since moving erratically makes you harder to track.

Avoid open "fire lanes" where a sniper can get a clear shot from a distance. Cover and concealment are your friends. (Cover is physical protection; concealment is darkness and camouflage.) If caught in the open, get low and crawl like a snake.

93 Slip Past Enemy Forces

If you're caught behind enemy lines, your goal is staying alive as you make your way to friendly forces.

SIT TIGHT Sometimes all you'll have to do is lay low and wait a while for the battle lines to shift, and you will end up surrounded by friendlies.

BE WARY If you feel you have to move, don't hurry, or you'll make mistakes and give yourself away. Avoid normal travel routes, because they'll be watched. Go on foot for silence and flexibility. Above all, avoid lines of conflict.

BE INVISIBLE Travel at night in dark clothing and without a flashlight. Look around before going out and move only when it feels safe to do so.

GET NOTICED If you know the good guys are near, signal to them in broad daylight. Wave a white flag (or underwear). Then come out with your hands up.

94 CASE STUDY: GONE POSTAL
Survive a Workplace Shooting

Standing outside on his break, Dave Ciarlante saw a coworker, Yvonne Hiller, walk purposefully into the Kraft Foods factory in Philadelphia, Pennsylvania. All he knew about her was her first name and the fact that she worked on the second floor. When he went back inside, a panicked security guard told him that Hiller had a gun. Ciarlante made a decision to help if he could.

As he ran upstairs after Hiller, he had no idea she had already claimed her first victim and was on her way to find others. When he came face to face with her, she told him to get out of her way. He moved aside, saying only that she didn't have to do what she was doing.

After she brushed past him, Ciarlante followed her. He took advantage of any cover he could find, ducking behind pillars or into alcoves and relaying details of Hiller's mission to supervisors and security personnel on his walkie-talkie. That communication allowed Kraft management to clear out employees in Hiller's path before she arrived.

Hiller was aware that he was following her, and she stopped frequently to confront him. Ciarlante's response was simply to remind her that he wasn't trying to stop her.

That tense standoff was shattered when one of Hiller's terrified coworkers rushed around the corner. Ciarlante yelled for the woman to get away, warning her that Hiller had a gun. Hiller turned and fired at Ciarlante, who turned sidewise and ducked into a doorway, sure he'd been shot. The bullet, however, missed, and Ciarlante was able to continue relaying vital information to authorities. Hiller fired at others, but no one else was killed once Ciarlante chose to step in.

When Hiller locked herself into an office, Ciarlante directed police to the room where she'd holed up, and the deranged woman was taken into custody. Given the enormous size of the plant, Ciarlante's courage, knowledge of the factory layout, and use of his trusty walkie-talkie saved lives and helped law enforcement officials end the rampage.

Gone Postal

When Dave Ciarlante saw an armed coworker enter his workplace, he chose to put himself at risk to save others. By radioing intel to his supervisors and security personnel, he helped dozens of workers make their way to safety. Here's how his survival know-how measures up.

> ✔ Ciarlante knew his coworkers. His knowledge of Yvonne Hiller and of her workstation location tipped him off to where she was headed.

When Hiller confronted him, he moved out of her way. Instead of trying to overpower her, he shielded his face with his arms, and told her she didn't have to carry out her plan and that he was not trying to stop her.

When the shooter passed by, Ciarlante understood that she was not firing indiscriminately: She was looking for specific individuals. So he opted to follow her.

He didn't confront the shooter, instead shadowing her from a safe distance.

He used his walkie-talkie to relay Hiller's position to security guards and police officials, allowing them to warn other workers of the danger.

He warned any coworkers he saw about the situation, gave them instructions on where to go, and then continued to follow Hiller without confronting her.

When she turned her gun on him, he turned away quickly. The distance between the two—and the fact that he turned to the side and ducked into a doorway—meant that she missed her shot.

When police arrived, Ciarlante knew which office the shooter had hidden in after her rampage. He quickly identified the location for the officers, saving vital time that otherwise would have been spent searching the enormous complex—and possibly allowing Hiller to escape.

> ✖ Despite the fact that he was unarmed, Ciarlante chose to follow someone that he knew was homicidal and packing a gun. That seldom turns out well, and I can't recommend it.

CHECKLIST
Stock Your Gun Safe

Whether you need to hunt for food or fend off a home invader, a gun can come in handy. Since different situations call for different kinds of firepower, it helps to know your options.

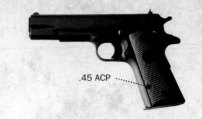

.45 ACP

HANDGUNS

☐ For home defense, a .45 ACP (automatic colt pistol) is a good choice for its reliability and power at stopping whatever it hits.

☐ A .44 revolver won't jam and provides heavy stopping power, so it's great as a backup firearm on hunting trips.

☐ Handguns in .22 or .38 calibers tend to be small and are ideal for concealed carry.

☐ A .410/.45 packs a double whammy: It can fire precisely-aimed .45 ammunition as well as .410 shotshells that have a large spray, all while allowing you to keep the gun close to you and out of enemy hands.

.44 Revolver

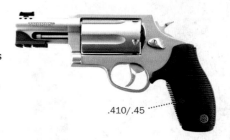

.38

.410/.45

LONG GUNS

☐ A .308 (7.62 x 51 mm) rifle with 3-to-9-power variable scope is mainly used for hunting, especially targeting large game.

☐ A great option for hunting small game, a .22 or .223 rifle won't destroy the meat or ruin the pelt.

☐ A 12-gauge shotgun provides versatility for taking down large game, such as deer, and smaller targets, such as geese.

☐ A 20-gauge shotgun is great for small-game hunting in thick brush or branches that might deflect a rifle bullet.

.308

.22

12-Gauge

20-Gauge

Combination Gun

Tactical Shotgun

AR Rifle

☐ A combination gun has a rifle barrel on top and a shotgun barrel on the bottom, giving the benefits of both a small-game rifle round and a shotshell capable of knocking down small game and fowl.

☐ Tactical shotguns make the best home-defense weapons, since their wide spray of pellets makes precise aim less necessary.

☐ An AR rifle, if legal in your area, is less unwieldy than a shotgun, allowing you to maneuver with ease and still shoot off multiple rounds.

96 Clean a Firearm

Start by removing any ammunition from the gun. Soak a rag with a gun-specific solvent, then run it down the inside of the gun's barrel, or bore. Allow three to five minutes for the solvent to loosen deposits. Next, run a solvent-soaked brush down the barrel, working it back and forth. Follow with dry patches until they come out clean. To finish, moisten a patch with three or four drops of gun oil and run it down the barrel.

97

Lock Up Your Weapons

Nothing's more dangerous than a gun that can fall into the wrong hands. The most secure method for storing guns and ammunition is to use a locked gun safe. Gun safes are too heavy to carry off, and most thieves won't take the time to try breaking into them. For extra security, all safes need a combination lock.

Also, consider locking your firearm in a small safe mounted to your bed frame, which will give you immediate access in an emergency. A bed safe can hold a handgun, a tactical flashlight, and ammunition, while still being small enough to go unnoticed.

98 Shoot with the Proper Stance

Set your sight and fire.

Angle your body toward the target.

Place one foot forward.

Shooting accurately begins with a strong stance and ends with a controlled trigger finger.

STAND LIKE A FIGHTER Stand sideways with your shoulder pointed toward your target. Move one foot slightly forward and lean just a little bit toward your aiming point.

GET A GRIP For extra stability, use a two-handed grip, wrapping your weaker hand over your stronger one. Grip the handle firmly but not as if you're trying to choke it, leaving your trigger finger relaxed. Position your trigger finger so that the crease of the first joint lightly makes contact with the trigger.

TAKE AIM AND FIRE Line up the front and rear sights with the target, then squeeze the trigger smoothly (rather than jerking it). The instant of discharge should be unanticipated, keeping your shot true to the target.

99

STEP-BY-STEP
Treat a Powder Burn

If you've discharged a weapon improperly by holding it too close to your body, or if you've been standing too close to a shooter, you could find yourself with a nasty powder burn. Here's what to do.

STEP ONE Start by flushing the burn with cool water or, better yet, cool saline solution, like what you would use for contact lenses.

STEP TWO To prevent infection, lightly cover the injury with a nonadhesive dressing and get to a doctor. Stitches or even grafting might be required.

STEP THREE If you can't immediately get to a doctor, at least apply some aloe vera gel, for crying out loud.

100 Deal with a Gunshot Wound

Gunshot wounds come in all levels of severity. Unless you're a doctor (and no, it doesn't count if you play one on TV), this is not the time to try your hand at surgery. Get help—but if you can't get it soon, you might have to take some steps.

If the bullet has passed through the gunshot victim, your job is to plug the holes to stop the bleeding and stabilize him or her. If the bullet is still in the body, leave it alone. If you're dealing with a shotgun injury, there will be numerous individual wounds to treat. There is really nothing to be gained by plucking out the shot, since disturbing the projectiles might cause more-serious bleeding or other damage. And if your tools aren't sterile, you might inadvertently introduce infection. So keep it simple: Stop the bleeding, dress the wound, and leave it to the doctors to remove the bullets and shot.

101

STEP-BY-STEP
Help Someone Who Has Been Impaled

One of your buddies got himself shot with an arrow or stuck with a spear. Now you're dealing with a victim who has been impaled by a sharp object. This sucks for you—but bear in mind that it's a whole lot worse for him.

STEP ONE Do not try to remove the sharp object. You could end up with a sucking chest wound or rapid bleeding out, in addition to internal tissue damage. The best you can do is try to stabilize the object so that it doesn't move while the victim is being transported.

STEP TWO If the impaling object is a long arrow or spear, carefully cut the length to make it easier to move the victim, leaving a bit protruding.

STEP THREE Pack the wound to stop the bleeding, then call an ambulance or drive the victim to an emergency room.

102 Silence Your Gun

The sound of gunfire can make you a target in a dangerous situation. If you want to cut those risks, make a quick and easy silencer and flash suppressor from an empty 0.5-gallon (2-l) soda bottle and a newspaper.

You'll want to start by cutting a hole in the bottom of the bottle that's about twice the diameter of the neck. Next, fit the bottle over the barrel of your rifle and secure it with electrical tape. Gather several sheets of newspaper and roll them up, then stuff the bottle with them. When you can't fit any more paper into the bottle, your sound and flash suppressor should be ready to go.

103 Modify Your Shotgun

Sawing off a shotgun is the easiest of all gun modifications, and one of the handiest: You might choose to resize a shotgun to fit a specific purpose (if, for instance, you have a small space to defend where a longer gun would be more difficult to maneuver). Or you might saw off a shotgun so that a smaller person can wield it without discomfort. Sawing off the damaged barrel of a gun might even make that weapon work again. (Just be aware that the lighter weight will result in heavier recoil.)

So go for it: Amputate the barrel with a hacksaw or other suitable blade. Be sure to clean up the cut with a file to make sure you haven't left the barrel at a weird angle and that there are no splinters or shards sticking up into the barrel. It's also a good idea to smooth away any imperfections in the cut surface with an emery cloth. Clean often to prevent corrosion.

104 STEP-BY-STEP
Make the Most of a Shotgun Shell

Sometimes what's inside a shotgun shell might be more useful to you than the shell as a whole. There's wadding inside that you can use as tinder. There's the shot, which you can melt down and form into another type of ammunition (shot is easier to work with than a slug, mind you). And, of course, there's gunpowder, which you can use to reload other shells—and it can also be useful in starting a fire.

STEP ONE Hold the shell by the brass end and use a knife to cut through the crimped end. Or pry the shell open with needle-nose pliers.

STEP TWO Once the crimp is open, turn the shell over and empty out the shot load.

STEP THREE Use your fingertips or a pair of needle-nose pliers to pull out the wadding.

STEP FOUR Turn the shell over again and dump out the gunpowder.

STEP-BY-STEP
Shoot a Crossbow

The crossbow is a medieval weapon that remains useful today. It has several advantages over firearms, two of which are stealth (it's much quieter than a gun) and reusable ammo (you can't fire a bullet more than once). Here's how to use one:

STEP ONE Place the crossbow stirrup on the ground and step on it to hold it in place.

STEP TWO Using steady tension, draw the bowstring back to its cocking mechanism. When it's secure, you'll hear a distinct click.

STEP THREE Place your arrow into the barrel and bring the crossbow up to aim. Hold it as you would a rifle, and use the bow's mechanical sights to find your target. The optimum distance is about 20 to 30 yards (18–27 m) away.

STEP FOUR Pull the trigger back smoothly to release the arrow. The crossbow will recoil, so brace yourself.

106

Sharpen a Knife

Some lessons learned in the kitchen can also prove useful in self-defense. And when it comes to survival, a sharp knife is crucial, so sharpen your knives on a regular basis.

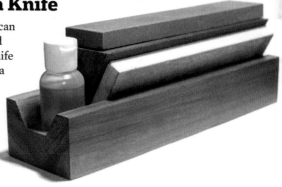

STEP ONE Use sharpening stones ranging from 300 to 1,200 grit. The lower the number, the coarser the stone and the rougher the finished edge. Applying a little knife lubricant to the stone will help the process.

STEP TWO Place the blade's edge on the sharpening stone at a 45-degree angle, and position the pad of your thumb as a spacer under the blade's spine, opposite the cutting edge.

STEP THREE Move the length of the blade across the stone as if you're trying to shave a thin piece off it.

STEP FOUR Turn the blade over and repeat on the other edge, holding the knife at a 45-degree angle.

Pick Your Blade

In choosing the right knife for your needs, the first decision is between fixed-blade and folding-blade knives. A folding blade collapses into the handle for easier carrying, while a fixed blade requires a sheath.

Look at two key areas: the knife point and the shape of the cutting edge. One of the most common types is the clip-point knife; the spine of the blade curves into a concave tip, making it ideal for piercing as well as cutting.

Clip-Point Knife

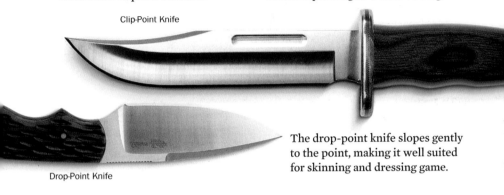

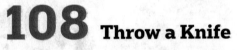

The drop-point knife slopes gently to the point, making it well suited for skinning and dressing game.

Drop-Point Knife

108 Throw a Knife

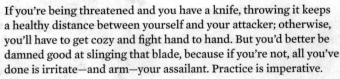

If you're being threatened and you have a knife, throwing it keeps a healthy distance between yourself and your attacker; otherwise, you'll have to get cozy and fight hand to hand. But you'd better be damned good at slinging that blade, because if you're not, all you've done is irritate—and arm—your assailant. Practice is imperative.

Grasp the knife by the unsharpened spine of the blade. Make sure you maintain a rigid wrist during the throw, as a floppy wrist results in uncontrolled rotation of the blade. Draw back the knife as your body rocks back slightly and your throwing arm reaches the cocked position. Then lunge forward and release the knife as if you were pitching a baseball. Learn to adjust your distance to accommodate the rotation speed so that the point penetrates the target.

Like I said, practice is key. Lots of practice.

109

Build a Better Bola

A bola (Spanish for *ball*) is a throwing weapon with three weights tied to the ends of three ropes. These ropes are then tied together on the unweighted end, forming a handle that allows you (hopefully with some skill) to throw the bola at an animal's—or a bad guy's—legs, binding and tripping in one motion. Here's a cheap and easy approach to making this effective short-range weapon.

STEP ONE Start with three tennis balls. Using a pocket knife or razor blade, cut two X-shaped holes on opposite sides of the ball.

STEP TWO Run the ends of a 3-to-4-foot (1-to-1.25-m) section of rope through both holes, tying an overhand knot at the exit point to keep the ball from falling off. (To guide your rope through the holes, try taping it to a straightened clothes hanger.)

STEP THREE Shove anything weighted into the hole. You can try using rocks, sand, or even spare coins.

STEP FOUR Overhand knot the other end of the rope, so that the ball is anchored at the rope's very end. Then wrap each ball in duct tape in order to keep the whole strand together.

STEP FIVE Knot the three unweighted ends together, and wrap in twine or more duct tape. To use your bola, just twirl it over your head and throw it as you would a lasso. After some practice, you'll be able to trip any bad guy that's dim-witted enough to come your way.

110 Make a Shank

You know the terms *shank* and *shiv* from prison movies. But until now, you probably didn't know how to make these do-it-yourself knives.

Shiv is slang for *knife*, and it includes anything that's already sharp or has a cutting edge, such as a razor blade. An old saw or a lawn mower blade makes for a perfect shiv. If it's dull, sharpen it against concrete, or use a metal file if you have one handy.

A shank, by contrast, repurposes a mundane item into a weapon. A toothbrush can be filed to a point, for example. A crude shank can even be made by folding a tin can lid in half. To make a handle, wrap a cloth strip around the shank's end.

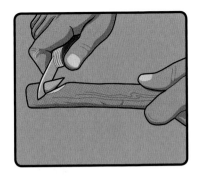

111

Make a Bow and Some Arrows

The bow and arrow was once the weapon of choice, and in a survival situation it will still serve you well. You'll need a piece of dry, dead wood about 1 yard (1 m) in length and free of knots or branches. The ideal wood should be fairly flexible, so choose mulberry or juniper, if possible. You'll also need some sort of material to use as a bowstring. This string can be hemp, rawhide, sinew, or rope. It's the wood that gives the bow its power, not the string.

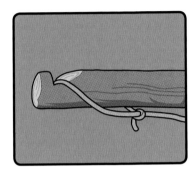

STEP ONE Cut notches at the top and bottom of the bow to hold your bowstring.

STEP TWO Tie off the ends of the rope in the notches. Your bow should have a slight bend to prevent it from snapping all the way back into a relaxed position.

STEP THREE For arrow shafts, select thin, straight rods of dry wood about half the length of the bow. Use any pointed object as an arrowhead.

STEP FOUR Use feathers for fletchings to balance the arrow in flight. Cut the feather down its center, then glue it (if possible) to the shaft, or tie it in place with a length of twine or light string.

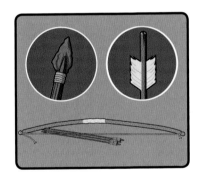

RICH SAYS
"Learn to view everything as a potential weapon, right down to the toothpick on your dinner table. I'm serious."

INDEX

About Rich Johnson

When it comes to survival, Rich Johnson has decades of experience. In the military, he was a paratrooper and demolition sergeant for the US Army Special Forces. In civilian life, he served as a Coast Guard Auxiliary instructor, and was an EMT and a firefighter for a volunteer fire and ambulance department. In his off hours, he has excelled as an advanced SCUBA diver, a sailor, and a backcountry skier. He specializes in urban survival, emergency preparedness, and primitive living techniques, and spent a year surviving in the desert wilderness with his wife and small children—part of which involved living in a cave and eating bugs (or anything else that moved). He's written extensively on survival topics for *Outdoor Life* and is the author of *Rich Johnson's Guide to Wilderness Survival*.

About *Outdoor Life*

Since it was founded in 1898, *Outdoor Life* magazine has provided survival tips, wilderness skills, gear reports, and other essential information for hands-on outdoor enthusiasts. Each issue delivers the best advice to nearly 1 million outdoorsmen. And with the recent launch of its survival-themed Web site, disaster preparedness and urban skills are now also covered in depth.

Credits

Cover images Front: *Shutterstock* (crowbar, background texture) Back: *Liberum Donum* (left, right) *Hayden Foell:* (center)

Photography courtesy of *Shutterstock* with the following exceptions: *iStock:* 28, 32 *Alexander Ivanov:* 107 *Knives R Us:* 62 *Dan Saelinger:* 95 (.308 rifle, 12-gauge shotgun, 20-gauge shotgun, AR rifle) *Taurus US:* 95 (.410/.45 pistol) *Windigo Images:* 96, 97

Illustrations by *Conor Buckley:* 22, 44, (icons) *Hayden Foell:* 11, 12, 68, 98, 108, 111 *Joshua Kemble:* 10, 13, 14 *Raymond Larrett:* 62, 151 *Liberum Donum:* 26, 29, Home Invasion, One Mean Machete, 109 *William Mack:* icons unless otherwise noted *Paula Rogers:* 38, 53 *Gabhor Utomo:* 44

Acknowledgments

Weldon Owen would like to thank Bridget Fitzgerald and Katie Schlossberg for editorial assistance, and Jenna Rosenthal and Sarah Edelstein for design help.

All of the material in this book was originally published in *The Ultimate Survival Manual,* by Rich Johnson and the editors of *Outdoor Life*. The original design for that book, adapted here, was by William Mack.

Disclaimer

The information in this book is presented for an adult audience and for entertainment value only. While every piece of advice in this book has been fact-checked and where possible field-tested, much of this information is speculative and highly situation-dependent. The publisher and author assume no responsibility for any errors or omissions and make no warranty, express or implied, that the information included in this book is appropriate for every individual, situation, or purpose. Before attempting any activity outlined in these pages, make sure you are aware of your own limitations and have adequately researched all applicable risks. This book is not intended to replace professional advice from experts in survival, combat techniques, weapons handling, disaster preparedness, or any other field. Always be sure to follow all manufacturers' instructions when using any and all equipment featured in this book. If your equipment's manufacturer does not recommend use of the equipment in the fashion depicted in these pages, you should comply with the manufacturer's recommendations.

You assume the risk and responsibility for all of your actions, and the publisher and author will not be held responsible for any loss or damage of any sort—whether consequential, incidental, special, or otherwise—that may result from the information presented here.

OUTDOOR LIFE

VP, Group Publisher Eric Zinczenko
Editorial Director Anthony Licata
Senior Editor John Taranto
Photo Editor Justin Appenzeller

2 Park Avenue
New York, NY 10016
www.outdoorlife.com

weldon**owen**

President, CEO Terry Newell
VP, Publisher Roger Shaw
Executive Editor Mariah Bear
Editorial Assistant Ian Cannon
Creative Director Kelly Booth
Senior Designer Meghan Hildebrand
Designer Diane Murray
Illustration Coordinator Conor Buckley
Production Director Chris Hemesath
Production Manager Michelle Duggan

© 2012 Weldon Owen Inc.

415 Jackson Street
San Francisco, CA 94111
www.weldonowen.com

Outdoor Life and Weldon Owen are divisions of

BONNIER

Library of Congress Control Number on file with the
publisher.

ISBN 978-1-61628-458-9

10 9 8 7 6 5 4 3 2 1
2012 2013 2014 2015

Printed in China by 1010 Printing International